GET READY TO READ

GET READY TO READ
A PRACTICAL GUIDE FOR TEACHING YOUNG CHILDREN AT HOME AND IN SCHOOL

TONI S. GOULD

ILLUSTRATIONS BY JO FAHRENKOPF

WALKER AND COMPANY

NEW YORK

Copyright © 1988 by Educators Publishing Service, Inc.
Revised edition copyright © 1991 by Walker Publishing Company, Inc.

This edition published in the United States of America in 1991
by Walker Publishing Company, Inc.

Published simultaneously in Canada by Thomas Allen & Son
Canada, Limited, Markham, Ontario

Library of Congress Cataloging-in-Publication Data
Gould, Toni S.
Get ready to read: a practical guide for teaching young children
at home and in school / Toni S. Gould: illustrations by Jo Fahrenkopf.
p.   cm.
Rev. ed. of: Reading, the right start. © 1988.
Includes bibliographical references (p.) and index.
ISBN 0-8027-7361-3
1. Reading (Preschool)—United States.   2. Reading—United States—
Parent participation.   3. Reading games.   I. Gould, Toni S.
Reading, the right start.
LB1140.5.R4G68   1991
372.4′1—dc20   91-22623
                CIP

Printed in the United States of America

10   9   8   7   6   5   4   3   2

To Kathy with love

CONTENTS

Today, more and more emphasis is placed on the importance of children's learning experiences in their early years. These are crucial in aiding or hindering their later growth in learning. Success in learning to read gives children a feeling of competence in one of their first intellectual endeavors and develops in them an ever-increasing confidence in their ability to learn and to think. Difficulty in learning to read can have crippling effects on their ability and willingness to learn in the future.

Children *enjoy* learning to read when the experience is a challenge to their minds, when they understand—not memorize—every step in the learning process. In this way, their cognitive growth is significantly stimulated in the very process of learning to read.

Before children can learn to read, they have to develop certain skills. The idea prevailed in the 1940s and 1950s that such reading readiness would develop spontaneously around six or six-and-a-half years of age, and until that time children should be shielded from formal exposure to letters and numbers. Since the 1960s, however, we have come to know that reading readiness must be nurtured in young children by proper environmental stimulation—that readiness, in effect, can and must be taught.

The specific method I have used in teaching children to read, both as a consultant to inner-city school classes and with private pupils, is called Structural Reading. This approach, while not the only way of teaching reading, is a most effective way of teaching through insight, that is, through understanding structure. The structured sequence of its complete readiness program is suitable for all children. Its success, to a large extent, is due to the self-teaching materials; hence, children are able to make independent discoveries and correct their own errors.

Such self-teaching materials allow the teachers to withdraw to the periphery of the learning process and become facilitators. This is in exact accordance with the statement made by a National Education Board panel which stated emphatically that "teaching must come to mean helping children to learn."

How does Structural Reading differ from other teaching methods? In contrast to the sight or phonic approaches, its emphasis is on understanding the structure of spoken words. This approach does not depend on memorization, but on teaching the correspondence between sounds and letters according to a carefully graded, systematic sequence that enables children to figure out words on their own from the start. Spontaneous comments, taken down verbatim in classrooms or in private, one-to-one teaching situations, show that children enjoy learning to read when the learning process makes sense to them and allows for independent discovery.

Teachers and parents must understand the total learning-to-read process if they are to become knowledgeable as to which specific games or activities develop reading readiness and which do not. This book gives adults a general understanding of the dynamics of the learning process that underlies learning to read. Many books are available to help teachers and parents teach children to read, but very few, if any, explain how to develop reading readiness systematically, so children will be prepared to experience continuing success.

Get Ready to Read presents a step-by-step teaching sequence that leads children from general readiness activities to learning specific sound-letter correspondence, and eventually to reading their first words and sentences. Instructions for games and activities are included for use in classrooms that have been divided into small groups, or in one-to-one teaching situations.

From 1965 until 1968, I served as a reading consultant to the Deutsch Institute for Developmental Studies. Dr. Martin Deutsch obtained funds to establish four classes for four-year-olds and to pay for half of the salaries of four kindergarten and four first-grade teachers. (He also partially funded the salary of the existing kindergarten and first-grade teachers in those schools.) Each class was divided into three reading groups, and each group received between twenty and thirty minutes of instruction per day. Thus, more instructional time was provided per week than is usually possible in private tutoring.

From 1968 until 1970, I was part of a research project funded by a Department of Health, Education, and Welfare grant at the Eighteenth Avenue School in Newark, New Jersey. A first-grade control group was taught by a basal reading approach; I was the consultant to the experimental group taught by Structural Reading. The second year of the project, two new first-grade classes and two kindergarten classes (the latter by request of the teachers) were started as experimental classes in addition to the original class, which was then in second grade.

In each of the four-year-olds' classes and kindergartens we were able to put into action a structured readiness program that developed every readiness skill, including sound-letter knowledge. There was no pressure to reach definite goals. The children's achievement varied from mastering six letters successfully to reading by the end of kindergarten. All but one of the first graders were reading fluently by the end of the year. The bright first graders, in Newark as well as in New York City, started their second grade Structural Reading workbooks by the end of April of first grade.

For the past ten years, I have been using the two previous editions of this book as a text in my reading course at the Bank Street College of Education in New York. To my delight, I have found that elementary school teachers of all grades, and even junior and senior high school teachers have found this book useful. Not only do they want to know about the learning-to-read process and which skills it involves, but they also have many students who still need help in acquiring a basic foundation on which to build their reading skills. These teachers asked me to write down my experiences and suggestions as I presented them in workshops and in classes. I wrote this book, in part, for them.

This book will also be helpful for parents, but not for those who want to produce super-children who will blitz their peers. Rather it is intended for those parents who want to encourage their children in all areas, for those who want to challenge their children's minds without pressuring them to perform.

Just as there are natural musicians, there are children who seem to be natural readers; they push their relatives relentlessly to teach them to read. Obviously, these children would learn to read regardless of method or approach, but *how* they are taught in the beginning will greatly influence their intellectual development and their ability to think things through for themselves.

Other children do not push to learn at an early age. They may have been late talkers, slow in handling a pencil or brush, unable to remember the names of colors or to write their names. Some have a tendency to form certain letters backwards. These children should be helped early also. Allowed to develop reading readiness skills at their own pace, they will experience success in an area where they might otherwise meet with failure.

This book presents case studies of children with serious learning disabilities who were referred to me before they went to kindergarten. Their comments show their confidence in their ability to learn. They demonstrate how an early start can prevent later failure.

This book was originally called *Home Guide to Early Reading with Reading Readiness Games and Exercises for Your Preschool Child*; it was written for parents. A new version was then brought out: *Reading—The Right Start*, intended for both parents and teachers.

In this third, updated version called *Get Ready to Read* I am addressing preschool, kindergarten, and first-grade teachers, as well as parents. This time I have included more excerpts from recent records of pupils with learning disabilities, and I have added more suggestions for helping such children learn; I also added more of my consulting experiences with disadvantaged children in classrooms. At every level, the results in terms of reading achievement and rise in self-esteem were most rewarding. Finally, I added a brand new chapter for parents (chapter 5).

ACKNOWLEDGMENTS

Until this book, my mother, Catherine Stern, and I collaborated on every project. I learned from her not only how to teach children arithmetic and reading, but also that children enjoy learning and grow in mental stature when challenged intellectually. I am grateful to her for having allowed me to modify the Structural Reading Program into a book for teachers and parents. My mother died long before this book went to press, but she read the original manuscript and penciled in some corrections.

Deep-felt gratitude goes to Jean Read whose master touch is visible everywhere. Her instant grasp of what I wanted to say, her insistence that I say it as succinctly as possible, and her rare gift for cutting unnecessary details all improved the book immensely. Working with her was an intellectual pleasure as well as a challenge.

I am very grateful to Diane Winkleby who improved the first revision greatly with her thoughtful suggestions and incisive editing.

I am indebted to Ely Porras-Gould, my daughter-in-law, who edited and typed parts of this manuscript conscientiously and skillfully.

Mary Kennan Herbert, my present editor of this book, has, from the very start, guided me with most helpful suggestions. It is a great feeling to know that, as the book goes to press, it is in the hands of an expert and wise editor. Thanks!

To protect my pupils, I have changed their names and sufficiently altered each family situation, so that they cannot be identified. However, the essential part of the records and all of the children's comments are reproduced verbatim. It was a challenge and a joy to observe these children, and I often learned as much as I taught. Their parents, through their cooperation and support, did much to make the job easier and more productive.

I am grateful to my sons Tim and Jeff for helping me with difficult issues and/or suggesting solutions. I want to thank my daughter Kathy for her encouragement, her willingness to discuss learning and teaching problems, and her subtle yet steady insistence that I not give up working on this book.

GET READY TO READ

1
Learning Through Insight

Bruce, age four, who had just completed some informal reading readiness tests, lingered at the door of the study. When asked what he wanted, he said, "I don't want to go. I came to learn to read today."

While Bruce's optimism goes beyond the realm of possibility, it is a perfect example of the very strong motivation that most young children have for learning to read. All children start out with a healthy, boundless curiosity to investigate the world about them, and this curiosity includes wanting to know what those strange squiggles on signs and in books say.

We grown-ups make an arbitrary distinction between learning and playing. Children do not. From the time that young children watch older siblings and adults around them pick up books and become absorbed, they want to learn to read. To them this is a skill that provides the entrance ticket to the grown-up world. Because of their spontaneous interest, learning to read, while not accomplished in one day, can become the most challenging and thrilling adventure in their lives.

Reading is generally agreed to be *the* single most important skill a child can possess. It is the one that is taught earliest and continued longest. What is often overlooked is that teaching children to read is fascinating for teachers as well as parents, and not that difficult. The crux of the problem is to find ways of teaching that will capitalize on the child's natural interest.

Unfortunately, reading experts do not agree on what kind of reading approach is best suited to capture children's interest. At this point, let's have a look at the teaching of reading from a broad frame of reference—namely that of the psychology of learning and teaching. After we have established some criteria for what constitutes the best learning conditions, we can apply these to the specific problem of learning to read. What kind of learning captures children's interest and motivates them to pursue an activity?

Psychologists agree that basically two kinds of learning exist: learning through understanding and learning through memorizing. Learning through understanding is a challenge to children's intelligence; learning through memorizing is merely a demand on their memories. Children are excited when they are able to figure out a problem on their own.

Max Wertheimer, who founded the School of Gestalt Psychology in Berlin in 1913, developed the theory that learning by insight is not only more productive than learning by memorizing, but also more enjoyable for the pupil as well as the teacher. "Every good teacher enjoys teaching and learning when really sensible learning takes place: when eyes are opened, when real grasping, real understanding occurs, when the transition takes place from blindness or ineptness to orientation, understanding, mastery, and when, in the course of such happenings, mind develops."[1]

Most teachers and parents will be able to recall incidents from everyday life that illustrate children's excitement when they first grasp a new idea. The stories that follow happened in nonteaching situations.

> Peter, age four, was perched on a stool, playing at the kitchen sink. He poured water into an empty milk bottle. Then he stuck a cork into the bottle. When he wanted to retrieve the cork, it would not come out. He turned the bottle upside down: the water poured out but not the cork. He stood there, angry and confused. Almost absentmindedly he turned the bottle right side up and turned on the water. The bottle filled and overflowed. Out came the cork. Peter's face lit up. "Oh!" he exclaimed excitedly.
>
> For the next half hour Peter repeated the experiment. No one could entice him away from the sink.

While Peter's solution to the problem was accidental, he was thrilled with his achievement. The excitement generated by his discovery motivated him to repeat the experiment over and over again. He was learning through insight.

Children do not enjoy memorizing ready-made answers. They prefer to learn when they are active participants. Understanding how something works produces a feeling of achievement in children.

---

[1] Max Wertheimer, Foreword to G. Katona, *Organizing and Memorizing* (New York: Columbia University Press, 1940).

Beth, age three, sat down in front of a counting board, which had different-sized blocks and slots to match. Taking out the blocks was easy for her, but putting each block back into its proper groove was difficult. "This doesn't go," she said to herself. "Too big." She kept trying to fit the block into different places until she found the proper groove for the block. She had relatively little difficulty with the smaller blocks, but it took a lot of experimenting to find the right place for the longer blocks. Once, she stamped her foot, muttering, "It sticks out." Eventually each block was in its place. Beth beamed. She immediately took out all the blocks and started the game over again.

Beth understood the task; hence, she was able to correct her errors. When she played the game again, she could find the proper groove for each block more quickly. Her sense of achievement was written all over her face.

In recent years, various psychologists have stressed the importance of learning through understanding. Drawing conclusions from their own extensive and impressive research, they have pointed out that the quality of early learning experiences affects children's cognitive development. And their findings show that learning through understanding is far more effective than learning through memorizing. Jerome Bruner, former head of the Center for Cognitive Studies at Harvard University, has clearly stated that all children learn better if they "understand structure . . . in short, learn how things are related."[2]

Admittedly, some subject matter that has no structure cannot be understood. By its very nature it can only be learned through memorization. Whenever we are dealing with names of things or with isolated facts—facts that exist without inherent logic—we cannot learn them through understanding. The capital of Florida, how many people live in New York City, or the exact year in which the United Nations was founded are facts that can be learned only through memorizing.

In other areas of knowledge, facts are related. They are part of an understandable, logical design. School subjects such as arithmetic and geometry have structure, and children learn these subjects better if they are led to understand this structure. Grasping a general principle results in an economy in learning; there is *less* to learn.

Learning by insight is a far more productive way of learning than

[2]Jerome S. Bruner, *The Process of Education* (New York: Vintage Books, 1963), p. 7.

is mere memorizing, for it produces transfer. Transfer means that children are able to apply their learning to related tasks. Instead of having to rely on the teacher to provide every answer, children are able to figure out answers on their own.

Learning by insight also has a positive effect on ability to remember. While children should not learn through blind memorization, they must, of course, be able to remember what they have learned. Remembering is easier when children understand the underlying structure and can thus reconstruct a given fact. Jerome Bruner stresses this point in beautifully concise terms. "An unconnected set of facts has a pitiable short half-life in memory. Organizing facts in terms of principles and ideas from which they may be inferred is the only known way of reducing the quick rate of loss of human memory."[3]

Making mistakes is natural in any learning situation. However, errors that happen because learning has occurred by rote memorization are the occasion for a decrease in efficiency of learning and in motivation. When a teacher says "wrong!" children not only feel diminished, but they often acquire lasting feelings of uncertainty. When they encounter this same fact again, they feel helpless, in effect saying to themselves, "I can't remember which answer was wrong and which was right."

On the other hand, when children learn by insight, errors assume a useful function: children are able to learn from their errors. The errors become the occasion for more learning, and this gives children increased confidence that they have now mastered this particular area of difficulty. An example from the teaching of arithmetic will clarify this last point.

> Lisa, age eight, came in for her weekly lesson, very upset. "I'll never get the zero facts, never." She handed me the test she had taken at school on which she had done very poorly. The first row looked like this:
>
> $$6 \qquad 7 \qquad 3$$
> $$+0 \qquad \times 0 \qquad -0$$
> $$\overline{0} \qquad \overline{0} \qquad \overline{0}$$
>
> "I just can't remember when the answer is zero," she added in tears. I put aside the test and gave Lisa a block that was four units long. The following dialogue took place:

---

[3] Bruner, *The Process of Education*, p. 31.

Mrs. G.: "Add nothing to the four-block. What do you have now?"

Lisa: "I still have the four-block."

Mrs. G.: "Take nothing away from the four-block. What do you have now?"

Lisa: "I have the four-block."

Mrs. G.: "Let's write down what we just did." Together we recorded the two arithmetic examples. Lisa filled in the answers completely on her own.

$$4 + 0 = 4$$
$$4 - 0 = 4$$

Mrs. G.: "Now give me zero times the four-block."

Lisa: "You don't get anything if I give it to you zero times. That's not giving it." Together we recorded that fact as

$$4 \times 0 = 0$$

We repeated the experiment once more with a different block, and then Lisa made up some examples on her own while I copied over the test she had taken in school. At the end of the lesson I gave Lisa the test. She solved every one of the examples correctly. "I got it," she beamed. "They can't trick me again."

To summarize: We have seen that learning through understanding produces the best learning conditions. It results in transfer and discovery because facts can be reconstructed easily and reliably, and it gives errors their sensible function of increasing rather than decreasing understanding. Such success in learning directly affects the learner's motivation; it heightens the interest that already exists.

It follows that in the specific area of learning to read, children should also learn through understanding, not through memorization. The crucial question is, *How* do they learn to read? Do the children understand every step in the learning process? Are they able to participate actively in the learning process? Are they able to make discoveries on their own, independent of the teacher? In the process of learning to read, do they use and stretch their minds or merely train their memories?

Having established some criteria for how children learn most productively, let us apply them to some different approaches to the teaching of reading. Historically, and speaking of this century only, the phonics approach came first.

KEY TO SOUND-LETTER CORRESPONDENCE

/m/

Throughout this book a letter inside diagonal lines refers to its sound when it starts a word. For instance, it refers to the initial sound of the spoken word /man/, a brief "mmm" sound without any vowel following.

m

All italicized letters refer to the printed form of the letter and children should be taught to pronounce their sound names, not their alphabet names. Chapter 9 shows how to teach children to respond to the printed letter *m* by its sound /m/.

ă, ĭ

A breve above above a vowel means you give its short sound, the sound you hear in *ăpple* or *ĭnk*.

ā, ī

A macron above a vowel means you give its long sound, as in *cāne* and *pīne*.

In the old-fashioned phonics approach, a teacher wrote a letter such as *m* on the chalkboard and informed the class, "This letter says /m/." The children obediently chorused /m/, attempting to glue a meaningless name to a meaningless visual configuration. After the class had memorized the sound names of all the letters of the alphabet, they were taught to put the sounds together to form words.

This next step was usually drilled in a two-step blending process:

$$m + a = /m\breve{a}/ \qquad ma + n = /m\breve{a}n/$$

This blending process was so difficult that children often called the sounds "/m//ă//n/" without comprehension. Although they arrived at the pronunciation of the single sounds, they failed to achieve the next important step of connecting the sounds with the spoken word. Thus, they did not complete the reading act, for they did not succeed in putting the printed word into the context of living, spoken language. Reading without comprehension is not reading. Unfortunately, many modern phonic approaches also use the two-step blending process which so often prevents children from understanding the meaning of a word.

There is no doubt that knowing the sound names of the alphabet gave children a useful tool for sounding out words. However, the learning process by which they acquired this tool was unproductive; they had to memorize twenty-six separate letters as isolated configurations without reference to meaningful, spoken language. The learning process did not provide them with sensible clues that would enable them to figure out a letter's sound by using their intelligence. They could master the names of the letters of the alphabet only if they had good memories. Nor did the next phase, learning to blend sounds, allow for learning by insight. Adding up letters in piecemeal fashion did not give children insight into the structure of written words. Because the drill on separate sounds was mechanical, children very often did not even grasp that a written word stands for a spoken word, that reading is, in essence, listening to the written word instead of the spoken word.

Because learning through memorizing is difficult and the rate of forgetting is high, as we know from the previous discussion on learning, a great deal of drill was necessary to fix the letter knowledge and blending in children's memories. In most classrooms the phonics instruction was administered very much like bad-tasting medicine. Many children learned in spite of the tedious drill, but they did not experience the enjoyment associated with learning to read.

Around 1930, the American reading specialist William S. Gray and his followers, determined to rescue children from this old-fashioned phonics drill, designed the sight method as a sensible approach that would center on comprehension as the focal point of reading instruction. They based their theory of reading on the following observations.

Mature readers do *not* pay attention to individual letters; instead they look at whole words, attaining the meaning instantly. It seemed sensible, then, to use the mature reader's performance as a guide for teaching the beginner. Gray and his colleagues believed that reading instruction should start with sight reading of whole, printed words, so that from the very first moment, the beginning reader would experience that reading consists of acquiring *meaning* from the printed word. This would make reading come alive and motivate children to want to learn to read more since they would no longer be subjected to meaningless drill.[4] This argument sounds seductively plausible un-

[4]William S. Gray and Bernice Rogers, *Maturity in Reading: Its Nature and Appraisal* (Chicago: Chicago University Press, 1956).

til we investigate *how* in actual practice children are taught to read by this method.

In the sight method, which is also called the look-say approach, the teacher writes a word like *city* on the chalkboard and pronounces it; the children *look* at it and then *say* it. They then take turns repeating the word.

The same teaching approach is followed when reading from a preprimer or a primer. The teacher tells the children what each word is, and they memorize what they are told. Although children know the spoken word, as the teacher pronounces it, they have no means of unlocking the printed word for themselves, for they have not learned the sounds of the letters.

In this beginning stage, single words are taught as if they have no relation to each other, as if they were *names* of visual configurations. Since memorizing names is difficult and the rate of forgetting is high, this beginning vocabulary must be repeated over and over again.

Advocates of the sight approach realize the difficulty of memorizing the visual configurations of a great number of words and therefore advocate helping children's memories by providing additional clues. The teacher draws attention to the particular configuration of each word as one aid to memory and encourages the children to guess at a word using the accompanying picture or the context of the sentence or story as a clue.

After about fifty sight words have been introduced, the teacher gives children phonic clues. But this phonics instruction is not a systematic teaching of all the letters; instead, phonics is taught as backup to the sight reading process. If, for instance, the word *mother* appears in the primer, the teacher explains in the ensuing lesson that *th* stands for the sound /th/. Since the phonic clues are handed out in piecemeal fashion—a lesson on initial consonants here, a lesson on final consonants there, then several lessons on vowels or word families—they are helpful only sporadically. Haphazard instruction of phonics does not provide the beginner with a secure and systematic foundation for accurate reading.

On the surface the sight method looks not only impressive but also attractive, for it surrounds children with a word-filled environment. They start out learning with a real book in front of them or by reading an experience chart. The magic of this "instant reading" is replaced by grim reality when the children themselves realize that they do not have a reliable tool for unlocking old and new words accurately. Ultimately they are penalized for the easy beginning because learning to read by sight has serious and far reaching disadvantages.

Guessing at a word in a primer or an experience chart does not interfere with comprehension. Children can get the gist of a relatively simple story without knowing exactly what each single word is. Yet guessing is a disastrous habit because it eventually has to be unlearned. Guessing at words may hinder children's ability to comprehend the exact meaning the author intended. By third grade, at the latest, work in all subjects requires precise reading. Misreading just *one* word has often prevented children from being able to solve an arithmetic problem or follow directions in a social studies text.

Since children who learn to read by the sight method do not achieve a consistent understanding of the structure of words, they are not able to transfer their reading knowledge to related words. Knowing the word *stop* does not automatically enable them to read the word *top* or the phrase *bus stop*. Memorizing one visual configuration is a help only in reading that particular word; experience shows that it does not give the clue to figuring out related words.

Since children taught by the sight technique usually cannot figure out new words on their own, they must ask what each new word is. Or, if they have misread a word, they depend on the teacher to correct their errors. But this very dependence eliminates the possibility of independent discovery and impedes their intellectual development. Furthermore, they miss out on the sense of achievement that results from learning by insight.

Terms like "attractive," "colorful," or "meaningful" are supposed to draw your attention to the context: they do not describe the learning process. In every variation of the sight approach, children learn to memorize the "looks" or "configuration" of a word without understanding the pieces that make up the structure of the whole word. In effect, the learning process underlying the sight approach is exactly the same as that underlying phonics approach: learning by rote.

So, although the sight method changed the surface appearance of learning to read, the basic learning process remained the same.

One dictionary gives the following definition of reading: "To apprehend accurately the meaning of the printed word." None of the nine dictionaries I studied uses the word guessing in their definition, thus excluding all those reading approaches which encourage guessing. The definitions also eliminate all phonics approaches which allow children to read a word, i.e. call a word, without understanding its meaning.

One of the outstanding researchers in the field of beginning reading opens her book with the following sentence: ". . . the ability to read words, quickly, accurately, and effortlessly, is absolutely critical to skillful reading comprehension."[5] The word "accurately" condemns all sight approaches, while the words "quickly" and "comprehension" caution us about phonics approaches.

Children themselves are acutely aware of how they are learning to read. Their comments reveal to an astonishing degree, that *they* know the difference between memorizing and reading.

Nancy, a first grader of two months' standing, came home early one afternoon.

"Nancy," her mother called from the living room, "I have time for you right now. Bring your book and read it to me."

"Mom," replied Nancy, materializing at the doorway with a big grin, "I left my book at school, but I can read it to you anyway."

Go, Go, Go.	Help Jane.
Go, Dick, Go.	Go help Jane.
Help, help!	Go, Jane.
Look, Dick.	Go, Jane, go.
Dick! Dick!	Look, Dick."

A seven-year-old pupil whom I had been tutoring wanted to borrow one of my books, but warned me, "I can't take *Green Eggs and Ham* because I memorized that when I was little."

Nicky (6:7),[6] who had been taught to read by the Structural Reading method at home, commented on his first two months of traditional first grade. "I don't get it. You and Granny taught me to read, but at school Mrs. X teaches us to pretend to read."

Many children do learn to read by the sight method, provided they have good visual memories. However, it has proven disastrous for children with poor visual memories. Research studies[7] have con-

---

[5]Marilyn Jager Adams, *Beginning to Read: Thinking and Learning about Print* (Cambridge: MIT Press, 1990), p. 1.

[6]Throughout this book, numerals in parentheses after children's names denote their ages. The numeral before the colon refers to the year; the one after the colon denotes the months. The months are noted because significant changes can occur in less than a year with preschool and primary school children.

[7]Katrina de Hirsch, Jeannette J. Jansky, and William S. Langford, in their book *Predicting Reading Failure* (New York: Harper & Row, 1966), have come up with the fascinating results that intelligence as measured by an IQ score "ranked only twelfth among predictive measures" of subsequent success in learning to read; eleven other kindergarten tests, the majority of which appraised some aspect of visual memory, were better predictors.

firmed that it is good visual memory that counts in learning to read, and children without this, no matter how bright, may be doomed to failure. Their intelligence is no guarantee that they will be able to learn to read.

However, whether or not intelligence is made use of in learning to read is determined to a great extent by the "how" of teaching. A method of teaching reading that is based on rote memorization forces children to learn by rote; they have no other options. Not all of us are endowed with the gift of visual memory; yet in the sight method, visual memory is all-important, and bright children, like others, are forced to rely on it. They are given no opportunity to use their reasoning.

Paradoxically, children who are the most intellectually capable often fail to learn to read because they are not taught so that they can use their intelligence to learn. This unnecessary failure invariably results in emotional damage and further learning problems.

The sight method may have brought changes to the *appearance* of the learning situation. But the real solution is to change the dynamics of the learning process from within so the beginning reader can learn to read through understanding.

Let's look at the task of the beginning reader. The learning process of the beginning reader is dynamically different from the performance of the mature reader, whose eyes sweep over a page taking in whole words at a time, comprehending words, sentences, and even paragraphs in a flash. The accomplished reader no longer needs to pay attention to the individual letters that make up a word.

But we cannot take the accomplished skill of the expert as a teaching model for the beginner. Expert skill is the end product of a learning process, one that the beginner has to learn from the beginning.

It is usually difficult for grown-ups to empathize with just what learning to read means to a child. We recognize familiar words instantly, without remembering how once, long ago, we had to decipher them. Perhaps a good way to dramatize the difference between two diametrically opposed approaches to reading is to present "words" with unfamiliar symbols.

Look at the two "words" in figure 1.1 for two minutes and then cover them.

Now pick out the two "words" from the list of eight words in figure 1.2.

Now, how did *you* determine which configurations in the list

Figure 1.1 Two sample "words" with made-up symbols

rqⱶneᴅ

ⱶeqᴄneᴅ

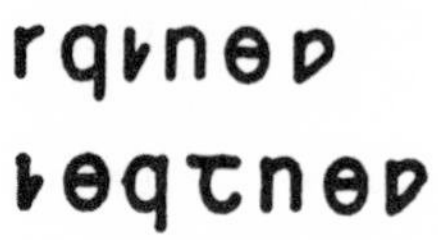

Figure 1.2 Eight "words" with made-up symbols

ᴡeqⱶneᴅ   ⑉oⱶneᴅ

ⱶeqᴄneᴅ   ⱶᴅqⱶn

rⱼ8uᴅe   rqⱶneᴅ

peᴅnqps   ᴅeqⱡⱼn8

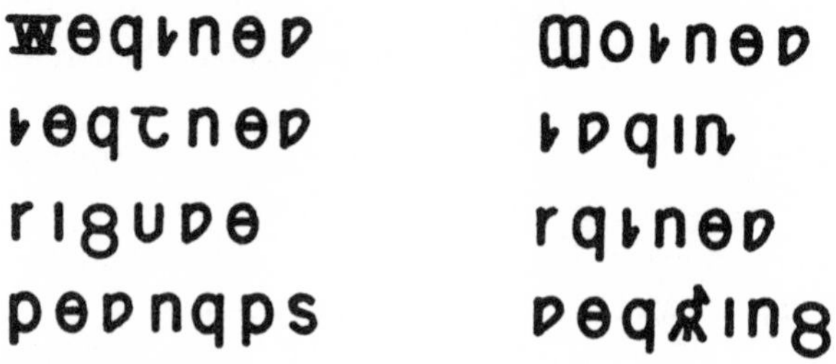

Figure 1.3 The symbols on the left represent the letters on the right.

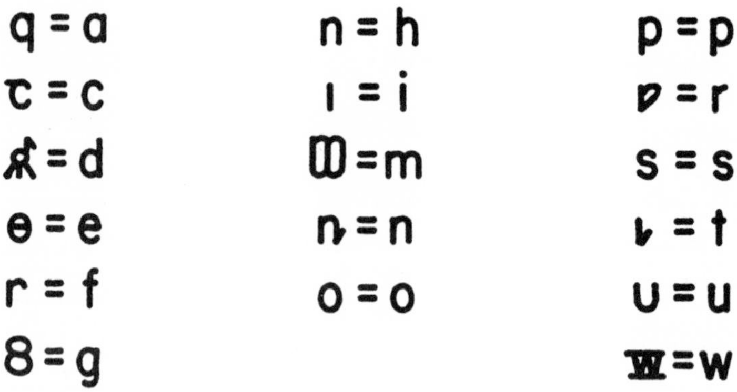

q = a	n = h	p = p
ᴄ = c	ⱼ = i	ᴅ = r
ⱡ = d	⑉ = m	s = s
ө = e	n = n	ⱶ = t
r = f	o = o	u = u
8 = g		ᴡ = w

were the same as the first two? Could you in any way reason it out? More likely, you relied on visual memory which, by the way, is far better developed in and far more experienced by the adult than by young children. But now, suppose I make it much simpler for you by giving you a code that will enable you to figure out each word? (See figure 1.3.)

You can easily *read* the words once you have the simple code. If

I changed all twenty-six letters of the alphabet into symbols, you could intelligently figure out any number of words under the same code. You can, of course, check back to the code while you are learning it, but you are not forced to depend on remembering each group of configurations as a whole. Compared to the beginning reader, you also have a head start because some of my code letters look familiar to you, and of course you do know how to read English. Children have to progress more slowly, but they, too, need a code so that they can figure out the letters intelligently rather than having to rely on an accurate visual memory of them.

Learning the twenty-six symbols of our alphabet is easier and far more productive than memorizing fifty unrelated sight words. The code of the alphabet unlocks accurately all of the regular words in the English language, and in no small measure, helps with the reading of irregular words.

The first major task of beginning reading instruction is to teach this code without turning back the clock to the outmoded phonics drill. We must find a way of teaching the code that allows for learning by insight so that pupils can participate actively in the learning process from the very beginning, using their intelligence, not their memories.

The second major task is to control the reading vocabulary presented to the beginning reader so that it reveals the structure of written language. This brings us to the third major approach to the teaching of reading, namely, the linguistic one. In 1942, Leonard Bloomfield, the American linguist who pioneered in the field of reading, challenged the sight method's rationale that the first reading vocabulary must present words that are in the child's speaking vocabulary. Many of these words are irregular. Bloomfield maintained that a beginning reading vocabulary with irregular words like *look, come, go,* and *to,* frequently found in primers using the sight approach, often confuses children.[8] Although these four words are commonly spoken by children, they have four different sound values for *o.* When children see another work with *o* in it, which sound value for *o* should they use?

Those experts who follow the linguistic approach believe that to be able to use the code successfully, that is, to learn to decode, beginning readers must at first be given only linguistically regular

[8]Leonard Bloomfield and Clarence L. Barnhart, *Let's Read: A Linguistic Approach* (Detroit: Wayne State University Press, 1961).

words, which follow a completely regular spelling pattern. Such words have a one-to-one relationship between sounds and the letters by which they are recorded, for instance, monosyllabic short-*o* words. In words like *hop, box,* or *dot, o* stands for the same sound. Children who now meet a new word, say *fox* or *log* or *mop,* will be able to decode it on their own, even if they have never been taught to read the particular word before.

Bloomfield's gigantic contribution lies in his reforms of the structure of the reading vocabulary. Unfortunately, he was so strongly opposed to a phonics approach that he would not allow any phonic elements in his teaching method. He and his followers were opposed to teaching the sound names of the letters of the alphabet and to any form of blending. Instead they insisted that the children be taught only the alphabet names of the letters.

In practice, a pure linguistic approach works as follows. The teacher puts the words *can, man, Dan,* and *fan* on the chalkboard and tells the children what the words are. The children repeat the words. If they don't remember what a word is, they say the alphabet names of the letters. But reciting the alphabet names "/cee/ /ay/ /en/" is actually a handicap, for they do not lead children to the spoken word /can/. Therefore, a pure linguistic program does not allow for learning by insight unless children are bright enough to make the transition from the alphabet names to the sound names of the letters on their own.

A fourth major approach to the teaching of reading is Structural Reading, a modified form of linguistics. It is linguistic because it presents only linguistically regular words in a highly structured sequence. It is modified because it insists on teaching the sound names of the letters of the alphabet as the easiest and most expedient tool in unlocking words. Teaching children the sound names of the alphabet gives them the code in a way that allows for understanding and independent discovery. Also, in such an approach, words are not taught as complete units. Instead, the teaching starts with an analysis of a spoken word into sensible parts and proceeds to the analysis of the structure of the corresponding printed word. In this way children do not have to depend on the teacher to read aloud a new word, but they are able to decode words on their own.

The practice of teaching the sound names of the letters and of only presenting regular words is very much in accordance with conclusions drawn by Jeanne S. Chall, a professor of education at Harvard, who investigated a great many research studies on beginning reading instruction. "The best results," she says, "probably come from using some control of spelling patterns and directly teaching their sound values. Indeed, this is what several of the new linguistic reading programs do—the Allen Reading Materials, *Sounds and Letters*, the *Programmed Reading Series*, and the *Structural Reading Series*."[9]

To be quoted by Jeanne Chall as one of the three reading approaches that achieves "best" results has been one of the most rewarding milestones of my teaching career.

A modified linguistic approach, such as Structural Reading, incorporates the valid features of existing teaching methods. It adopts from the phonics approach its theoretical premise that, in spite of its irregularities, English is a phonetic language. Since a definite correlation exists between the sounds of speech and the letter-symbols that record them, children must be taught this correlation as an indispensable tool in learning to read. It also incorporates the premise of the sight approach—that comprehension must be the focal point of all reading instruction, that reading at sight must indeed be its goal. Finally, it uses the linguistic innovation of controlling the beginning vocabulary on the basis of spelling regularity as the easiest and most efficient way of teaching children to decode.

The unique contribution of a modified linguistic approach to teaching reading is that it changes the dynamics of the learning process. The learning process is such that children can learn by insight into structure, apply their knowledge to new words, and correct their own errors. Early in the learning process they realize that reading does not allow guessing, but requires genuine mental effort to arrive at the accurate decoding of the word. Their comments show their understanding of what reading means at this initial stage.

> Bobby, at the age of five, read the word *is* for the first time. Asked to use the word in a sentence, he pointed to his head with a whimsical grin and answered, "Reading *is* something you have to figure out up here."

> When she first learned to decode, Robin (5:4) guessed from the picture that the word said *man*. When I silently pointed to the word underneath the picture, Robin sounded it out, "/Dă/-/d/. /Dad/! I thought it was a man from the picture, but it says Dad, so they mean Dad. I can read words. That is real reading!"

[9]Jeanne S. Chall, *Learning to Read: The Great Debate* (New York: McGraw-Hill Book Co., 1967), p. 118.

2
The Natural Reader

A little girl appeared at the door of her mother's study, stating firmly, "I want to have a reading lesson. *Now*! I want to learn to read." The mother, tired from a long day at work and not able to tune in so fast to her daughter's request, simply shook her head and said, "You will be four in three months. That's when we'll start. We don't start teaching reading in our family until children are four." The girl, ordinarily very amiable, insisted. Her mother refused with equal vehemence. Not until the girl sobbed bitterly, "But I want it now!" did the mother give in. The mother had been arbitrary and wrong. The child was ready and learned to read in less than six months.

The principal of a New York City school was experimenting with the Structural Reading approach in two of her first grades, but consistently put off teaching her own son to read at home and promised that he would learn to read in school. After six weeks in first grade he came home one day and confronted her in a cold fury: "You promised me I would learn to read in first grade, and I am not learning! We talk about pictures! What about your promise?" She brought him the first readiness book of the Structural Reading Series[1] and explained the first pages. At seven o'clock the next morning she woke up to hear him working on the sound names of the letters. In less than two weeks the boy asked for the second readiness book, which he finished on his own. He demanded the third book in the series and worked phenomenally fast, and with very little help went through it in less than a month. He was delighted about finally being able to read; his faith in his mother was restored, and no damage was done. But the mother herself felt that she had almost missed a crucial moment, and in retrospect, she realized that she

[1]Catherine Stern, Toni S. Gould, and Margaret B. Stern, *We Discover Sounds and Letters*, Book A-1 of the Structural Reading Program (New York: Random House, 1972). This book systematically develops all the reading readiness skills, which are a prerequisite to learning to read. It also teaches ten letters by their sound names.

probably should have started to teach him at four, when he was first interested.

From these two examples we can see that almost as crucial as *how* children should be taught to read is the question of *when* they should start learning to read. Here, too, teachers and parents are faced with conflicting advice. At one extreme are some experts in early education who are convinced that children are not ready to master this complex skill until they are at least six years old. At the other extreme are books such as *How to Teach Your Baby to Read*[2] that urge early and energetic drills designed to produce an infant reader in every playpen.

THE CRITICAL PERIOD

What we know about learning in general shows us that there are optimum times for children to progress intellectually and to develop basic skills. These have been referred to in professional literature as "sensitive," or "critical," periods. Trying to teach a skill before the critical period is wasteful and often frustrating for both teacher and student. On the other hand, waiting beyond the critical period is unproductive because the child's natural aptitude for achievement and growth has subsided.

Now let us apply this concept of critical periods to the field of reading. The peak of interest for some children obviously occurs much earlier than the majority of our schools allow for. Some five-year-old children—and of these, many first show interest at four—are so curious about "what the words say," are so eager to learn to read, that they cannot wait. There are natural readers, just as there are natural athletes, and you should not arbitrarily postpone their learning until they have reached a certain chronological age when they are presumably ready to be taught in school.

It seems logical and necessary that children who are fascinated by letters and words be taught when they are most eager to learn. Obviously the quality and quantity of learning will be greatest when they are most interested. Children who are natural readers signal by their behavior that they are ready to learn to read. Teachers and par-

[2]Glenn J. Doman, *How to Teach Your Baby to Read: The Gentle Revolution* (New York: Random House, 1964).

ents can learn to assess their behavior. Natural readers have many, if not all, of the following characteristics:

- Natural readers are very much aware of printed words. They notice the labels on cereal boxes and canned goods. While riding in a car they notice highway signs such as "Yield" and "Stop." When being read to they point to a word in the book and ask, "What does this word say?" or, "Does this word say 'Mom'?"
- Many, but not all, natural readers seem to have a phenomenal memory for printed words. If told that a word on a cereal box is "cornflakes," they remember it and read it with great delight every time they see it. Similarly, they'll remember the "Stop" sign every time they pass it. They'll recognize not only their own names in print, but also their friends' names.
- Many natural readers scribble constantly. In the literature they have been described as paper-and-pencil kids. They are always busy copying words such as the names of their friends or the days of the week. Their interest in written language manifests itself in their trying to master it through writing.
- Many natural readers show a high degree of persistence. They usually stick to an activity for a much longer time than do children of the same age. They go on long binges of interest. It is delightful to observe these children totally immersed in an activity, unaware of distractions. Their concentration span is obviously a great asset in an early learning-to-read venture.

The question of *when* to teach natural readers who show all the signs of readiness still has to be answered. The critical period is marked by the signs just mentioned, but it is also contingent on children's internal maturation. No matter how interested children seem, before a certain stage of maturation, readiness skills may be developed but reading itself should not be taught.

While it is impossible to give a precise chronological age at which all natural readers should be taught, the following guidelines do exist.

❑ Two- and Three-year-olds

Two-year-olds and three-year-olds are not ready to sit down and learn letters. They are intent on exploring themselves and the physical world, and they need many opportunities for their sensory-motor development.

No matter how interested these children appear in writing words, they should not be taught to write either letters or words because they are not mature enough to make the connection between the concrete and the abstract. The observation that children cannot think abstractly until they are about four is borne out by the eminent Swiss psychologist, Jean Piaget.

Piaget has made an immense contribution to the difficult task of evaluating children's readiness for learning by describing the successive stages in the young child's cognitive development. Two- and three-year-olds can react only to a concrete situation; they cannot reason beyond what they see. They are not capable of symbolic or abstract thinking. For instance, they cannot comprehend that bananas, apples, and oranges—so different in their appearance—have something in common: they belong to a specific group of food, that is, fruit. It follows that in the area of reading readiness, children cannot understand that different words like *mitten, mask, mirror,* and *magazine* have something in common: they belong to the group of words that start with the same initial sound, /m/. Since two- and three-year-olds are not able to think abstractly, specifically to classify, they are definitely not ready to learn the relationship between sounds and letters. Their intelligence is not mature enough to learn that skill.

Children as young as two or three can sometimes be taught a letter of the alphabet; for instance, they can learn mechanically, by rote, that the configuration *m* says /m/. Or they can be trained to respond to the printed word *toes* with the spoken word /toes/, an approach advocated by Doman. But such drill dulls rather than furthers children's intellectual development. Excitement and active participation in learning are absent when learning consists of repeating what the teacher or parent has said. It is wiser not to teach reading to two- and three-year-olds; it is better to postpone it until they can understand the learning process and are thus able to make independent discoveries such as figuring out a letter's sound or reading new words on their own.

However, curious two- or three-year-olds interested in language can be challenged in other areas. The most important is spoken, not written, language. These young children are intent on learning new words and concepts, and they are very proud when they use new and difficult words in their speech. Teachers and parents can help enrich their speaking vocabularies by talking to them, answering their questions, and explaining new words and concepts to them. The richer children's vocabularies become, the better they are prepared for reading, since reading comprehension builds directly on their comprehension of spoken language.

Reading aloud to three-year-olds can be a delight. After you have read a story, encourage children to talk about it. At this stage they are able to develop auditory discrimination. They can learn that a spoken word has an initial sound that they can hear and identify. Games that develop these skills are fun for young children and, at the same time, develop skills that need to be sufficiently practiced before a child can learn to read. (For a detailed description of these games, see chapter 7.)

❏ Four- and Five-year-olds

Children who show the signs of natural readers can learn best at ages four or five, provided the teaching method allows them to understand the process and make their own discoveries rather than learn configurations by rote.

Giving children the go-ahead at this stage has tremendous advantages. We teach them when they are most interested in learning and when they have the maturity to learn.

Children feel accomplished and competent—feelings they need to experience in *all* areas, not only in blockbuilding, painting, and clay-molding, but also in cognitive areas such as learning to read, write, and do arithmetic.

Recently, psychologists interested in the development of children's thought processes have stressed how important *early* learning experiences are in shaping children's learning for the rest of their lives. If they experience early that they can deal successfully with symbols, they will develop a feeling of competence. Children who are aware of using their powers of reasoning rather than the ability to repeat or memorize develop an image of themselves as thinkers. These early feelings about themselves, that they can deal with symbols, are crucial in their development as learners.

Teaching children at the optimum time constantly reinforces their intrinsic motivation. Very little, if any, outside pushing from the adult is necessary. The enjoyment of learning for its own sake is the single most important outcome of teaching children to read at their critical periods.

Having accepted the idea that children should learn to read at their critical periods rather than later in first grade when those periods may have gone by, you may ask, "Wouldn't it be better if children, obviously natural readers because of their compelling interests, picked up reading on their own? Is it wise to interfere with this natural process?"

Some natural readers *do* try to teach themselves. If they learn enough phonics to figure out the code on their own, they can become excellent readers. However, it is risky to let natural readers teach themselves, because on their own, they may learn to guess.

Guessing comes naturally to children who are impatient, for it is always easier and quicker than accurate decoding. Such children may read *String Beans* instead of *Whole Green Beans* on the frozen package in the freezer. Or on their way to a friend's house, they may read *Hill Street* instead of *Hill Avenue*. At this beginning level, when the children's guessing has no serious consequences, errors may slip by unnoticed. After all, children will bring the green beans to their parents, and they will succeed in finding their friend's house. Yet guessing may seriously interfere with children's learning in later years. For instance, it will prevent their understanding the exact meaning of a paragraph in a history book or from solving a mathematics problem that requires the accurate reading of every word.

Breaking a habit of guessing that has been practiced for years is very difficult. Once children think they can read, they will not be eager to relearn either from the teacher or the parent. At this point, reading instruction loses its original flavor of excitement and takes on the taste of remedial teaching.

It is wiser to teach children sound-letter correspondence *before* they learn to read words. This way they acquire the tools that enable them to read each word accurately.

At the other extreme from the guessers are natural readers who pick up a lot of phonics from an older sibling or friend and thus are able to sound out a great many words accurately. Because they have no idea what each single word means, they may fail to understand the sentence as a whole. Such word calling is as equally faulty as guessing and is also hard to unlearn.

There is another crucial reason why children should be taught systematically rather than allowed to teach themselves haphazardly. Reading and writing both have their natural roots in spoken language: children should learn simultaneously how to transfer listening to reading and speaking to writing. Each reinforces the other. For instance, the practice of tracing a letter helps children discriminate letters and insures the identification of each letter.

Some natural readers between the ages of four and five lack the eye-hand coordination necessary for writing. It is especially important for them to be taught this skill along with reading. Children at this age never tire of the games aspect of an activity and, through playing, develop eye-hand coordination and soon the writing skill itself. In first grade, however, they find it a boring chore to learn to write the letters of the alphabet. After all, they can already read books!

Spelling, too, should be part of this learning process. Here, we adults have to free ourselves of the notion that to spell a word means to be able to recite by rote the proper sequence of the alphabet names of the letters. Can children be said to spell the word *cat* only if they recite the alphabet names of the letters "/cee/ /ay/ /tee/"? Such a performance bears no resemblance to the spoken word /cat/. Think, instead, of spelling as a natural process, which also has its roots in spoken language. Children can say the name /cat/ out loud and, listening to themselves, can record the sounds they hear by writing the corresponding letters. (This presupposes that they have been taught the sound names of the letters.) Four- or five-year-olds find it intriguing that they can record a word they can pronounce, and in this way, spelling becomes a natural process of self-dictation, at least in the beginning of instruction (see chapter 10).

FIRST DISCOVERIES IN READING

If you are fortunate enough to be teaching pre-kindergarten or kindergarten or you are an interested parent, you can use the suggestions in this book to systematically provide the first learning experiences leading to learning to read. Don't think of this as a formal teaching assignment. Your task is to informally provide the proper learning environment for children to make their first discoveries in reading.

Now, what happens to children who do learn to read early? Are they bored in first grade? On the contrary. First graders who already know how to read are able to start reading books at a more advanced level, and naturally the more they read, the better they become. Early readers report years later how satisfying it was to read all the picture books in kindergarten, the birthday cards at parties, or the headlines in the daily newspaper. One first grader who found a letter in his desk from his mother, who had visited his classroom on parents' day, proudly refused the teacher's offer to read it to him as she would for the other children. "I already read it," he explained nonchalantly.

I have never received any criticism from a school or teacher about my early tutoring. All of the first grade teachers I have worked with have been most appreciative that children, with or without learning disabilities, came to first grade already knowing how to read, write, and spell.

Research has shown that these early readers keep their head start even after several years have elapsed. Dolores Durkin, professor of education at the University of Illinois, has been conducting studies on children who learned to read before going to school. She has concluded that "What the research findings indicate is that the average achievement of preschool readers, over as many as six school years, remains significantly higher than the average achievement of equally bright schoolmates who did not begin to read until after they started first grade."[3]

Even more important than their head start is that first-grade children feel competent and successful from the very minute they start school. Nothing succeeds like success, which is an intoxicating inspiration and catalyst that helps establish a positive cycle: from learning to motivation to more learning and heightened eagerness to learn. Such a cycle is vitally important because it shapes children's attitudes toward learning, and this can influence their success throughout their school years. Its importance almost equals the actual accomplishment of reading itself.

[3]Dolores Durkin, *Teaching Them to Read* (Boston: Allyn and Bacon, second ed. 1974), p. 156.

3
When to Begin

....

"You'll have to teach Bobby to read *before* he goes to school," Mrs. B. told me on the telephone. "He'll never learn once he's there. He's four and a half and he won't sit down with a puzzle. He doesn't even want to listen to a story."

I knew Bobby's family because I had tutored his two older brothers in reading. Both were above average in intelligence but had been handicapped by severe perceptual problems that gave them difficulties in school. I promised to take Bobby on a trial basis to find out if he was intellectually mature enough to learn to read. If Bobby's mother was right, it did seem sensible to give him a chance to learn to read *before* he encountered failure.

The mother's remark about her youngest turned out to be the understatement of the year. Bobby wouldn't listen, period. To any simple direction such as "Take a pencil," Bobby replied, "What?" It soon became obvious that this was his stock phrase. Every direction, expressed in simplest terms, was challenged by "What?" or "What did you say?" Even tempting questions such as "Would you like a cookie?" or "Would you like some punch?" received the same response.

Bobby was a restless child, and during each lesson some time was spent retrieving pencils and toys that "accidentally" fell on the floor. His mind wandered, too; he'd suddenly wonder out loud what his mother or his brothers were doing at home and when they were coming to pick him up. But he soon got used to the structured hour, sitting down, listening, and playing games, and within a few weeks, he appeared much less restless during the hour. I gave him *We Discover Sounds and Letters*, the first readiness book of the Structural Reading Series. Bobby was thrilled to be working in a real book. He would ask for "my book" as soon as he came into the study, and he was very proud of being able to do several pages each time he came.

Simultaneously, we were playing a lot of games. On the table there were little toys, such as a mouse, a lion, and an ambulance. Underlying these games was a teaching purpose: Bobby was learning that every toy, every object, has a name that starts with a sound that we can identify. *Lion* starts with /l/, *tiger* starts with /t/, *fan* starts with /f/, and so on. Bobby had to learn to listen to my directions carefully and to concentrate on their meanings. He also had to develop sufficient auditory discrimination to be able to identify the initial sound. In a word like *lion*, he had to learn to hear only the consonant sound /l/, not the alphabet name /el/, nor the consonant plus a vowel, such as /lə/. Bobby mastered the skill of auditory discrimination in about eight weeks, a longer time than most children his age take, yet it was excellent progress considering his low level of concentration.

At this point I felt confident that Bobby was going to learn to read and that these lessons were, at the same time, helping him learn to concentrate. Although he still responded to most directions with "What?" I no longer had to repeat them. I simply sat back and waited, and in a few minutes he would carry out the direction or answer the question. As Bobby's attention span notably lengthened with each visit, both pupil and teacher felt the glow of success.

Now Bobby was ready for the second stage of learning. He had to understand the concept that the spoken sounds we hear can be transcribed into letters. I showed Bobby a picture of a mask with the letter *m* embedded in it. (See figure 3.1.) He identified the picture as that of a mask. I explained that the dark lines superimposed on the mask form the letter *m*, representing the first sound heard in the word *mask*, that is, /m/.

Then I asked Bobby to say the name of the picture, mask, to trace the dark lines with his finger, and to say /m/. Bobby understood this

Figure 3.1 Letter picture of *mask* for the letter *m*

assignment; he was delighted to be able to trace the *ms* in his workbook. In the next lessons he learned the letters *f* and *l* in a similar manner. I placed the three other pictures with embedded letters in a rack on the table. When working in his workbook or playing new games using the written letters, Bobby could use these pictures as a reference. But when I removed them, he was unable to identify a single one of the three letters. The *m* by itself did not say /m/ to him. Chapter 9 will explain in detail how to play games using these and other letter pictures.

My Waterloo had come. After seven sessions of trying both old and new techniques, Bobby still could not identify any of the three letters. It is true that some children at this age, especially those with either a poor visual memory or a severe perceptual problem, take a relatively long time learning the difference between *f* and *l* since they "look alike" to them. But all the children I had taught up to this time had learned to identify *m* after a fairly short time since *m* has a strikingly different configuration from *f* and *l*.

Clearly, Bobby and I were getting nowhere, so I phoned Mrs. B. and suggested waiting six months to a year before we resumed the lessons. Mrs. B. was most unhappy. "Bobby is counting on his lesson tomorrow; he looks forward to it. Won't you see him and explain to him yourself that he can't come until he is older?" I agreed to do this, but I suspect that Bobby's mother told him that this was going to be his last lesson.

I was confirmed in this thinking when Bobby marched into my study the next day. To my surprise he identified *m*, *f*, and *l* without a mistake, demanded to learn the name of the new letter on the next page, and then asked for "more letters."

Apparently Bobby had enjoyed the lessons in the past and was determined not to give them up. I realized that Bobby's increased eagerness was not the only reason for his success in mastering the four letters. The past lessons had laid a good foundation, but Bobby had needed *more* time, *more* practice, and *more* patience to develop the skill of discrimination than anything in my previous teaching experience had prepared me for.

Something else dawned on me. Bobby had not been able to make the transition from recognizing letters embedded in their meaningful context, the letter pictures, to identifying the letters themselves—to see the curious squiggle of lines in a letter like *m* and hear that it says /m/. Obviously Bobby had a severe perceptual problem and we were, fortunately, correcting it in its early stages.

The young children whom I had taught previously had made this transition without any difficulty; but Bobby needed more time than I had allowed to overcome his learning disabilities. What was working for us was his heightened motivation and his increasing ability to concentrate and comprehend; now he could master a learning process for which he had not been ready before. When Bobby left, triumphant that he was coming back the following week and "all the time until I know how to read," he did seem to be a couple of inches taller!

The question many readers will ask is, Would Bobby have learned the letters more easily if he had waited until he was six years old? Certainly, there is always a strong temptation to claim that a child is "not ready." But when does a child like Bobby *become* ready? Does he grow ready by himself?

In every area of learning, ability to acquire a new skill is determined both by what goes on inside the child (maturation) and what goes on outside the child (environmental stimulation). Jerome Bruner, discussing early learning in general and not confining himself to reading readiness, states: "The idea of 'readiness' is a mischievous half-truth. It is a half-truth largely because it turns out that one teaches readiness or provides opportunities for its nurture, one does not simply wait for it. Readiness in these terms consists of mastery of those simpler skills that permit one to reach higher skills."[1]

So, too, in reading, readiness does not spurt forth by itself from a hidden well inside children at a given age. It is the outcome of both the maturation of their nervous systems and the stimulation they get from the world around them. Nor is maturation in itself enough to overcome certain deficiencies or stumbling blocks in preparing the ground for learning. So, we must teach children those "simpler skills" that will actively prepare them to learn to read successfully. In a nutritive educational environment—with the proper teaching sequence and appropriate materials that allow for a child's gradual learning through understanding structure—children's critical periods will occur sooner than they would if the children had been left alone without any instruction. The task of the educators is to adapt their teaching to the children's levels of learning so that in the process of learning, they will be prepared to tackle the progressively more difficult tasks that have to be learned. Viewed from this active concept

[1]Jerome S. Bruner, *Toward a Theory of Instruction* (Cambridge, Mass.: The Belknap Press, 1966), p. 29.

of readiness, critical periods in children's learning depend as much on the skill of the educator as they do on the unique interests of the children.

Bobby, whose perceptual difficulties suggested the immaturity of a much younger child, wasn't "ready" to learn to read, but he needed my help to become ready. It was particularly important that Bobby, as a slow learner, have an early start since he needed a great deal of time to develop all of the readiness skills. The structured situation of the lesson by itself did a lot for his readiness: since he enjoyed the games, he learned to sit still and listen. As he gradually progressed in learning, he experienced a feeling of achievement, which in turn sparked his interest and his motivation to learn. Thus, through playing and without any coercion he learned to learn, and in the process he became more mature.

At four and a half, Bobby's interest in learning to identify letters was apparent even when his actual learning had temporarily slowed down almost to a standstill because he had found playing games with me enjoyable. For instance, he enjoyed the Letter-Tracing Game, which provided him with the necessary tracing practice; he never realized that he was practicing the same three letters. At the age of six, or even at five, it would have taken Bobby just as long to learn the letters, but he would have become bored by the games and, worse, discouraged by his slow progress.

Since my experience with Bobby, I have repeatedly found that children with severe learning disabilities need a great deal *more* careful help than the usual children to develop the skills necessary for learning to read. Because their reading readiness needs a longer time to be developed, they especially need to be started early.

Robin, another pupil, also benefited from an early start. She was no better prepared for learning than Bobby when she was referred to me. My first two sessions with Robin showed that she was so restless that she could concentrate on a single game or activity for only five minutes; she had very poor visual discrimination; she had a marked tendency to reversals in copying even the simplest design or trying to follow any indicated direction with her pencil; and her eye-hand coordination was very poor. It was impossible to determine if her constant "What?" was due to poor auditory discrimination or to poor listening habits. Actually, the question remained an academic one for ten months, for I had to repeat every direction because she "did not hear it."

But hidden beneath all Robin's restlessness and inability to concentrate appeared a good analytic mind and a keen desire to learn. She paid more attention to a hard game than an easy one, so in the second lesson I introduced the letter picture for /m/. She was thrilled. "That's what Susan [her older sister] did last year!" However, it took Robin ten months to learn nine letters. Without the letter pictures many letters "looked alike" to her.

We played a great many writing and tracing games to help her get a kinesthetic feeling for the letters. We constantly thought up new games; for instance, she invented a telephone game in which, with the aid of a toy telephone, she would call me, announce that she had a package for me, and then deliver a *lion* in person. To make sure I realized I was getting the correct package, she would trace over the *l* on a prepared page, saying, "I brought you a *lion*, and so I am writing the *l* for you." As her interest increased during those ten months, her concentration span gradually lengthened.

Robin went away for the summer at the end of June. When she came back, she entered public school kindergarten and came to me twice a week as before. To my tremendous amazement, Robin had not forgotten any of the nine letters she had learned the previous spring. She spent only three months learning the next fifteen letters, although she did not entirely master them and frequently had to check their names with their letter pictures. I sensed that Robin was now very eager to get to "real reading." I expected Robin to progress slowly, in part because she had not achieved mastery of all the letters. However, this was not the case.

What makes Robin's record so fascinating is the complete discrepancy between her long, hard struggle in learning the letters—it took her thirteen months to learn the sound-letter correspondence—and her amazing progress once she discovered reading. Because she was not only very impatient but also lacking in self-esteem, I let her teach herself a great deal more than would be possible, for example, in a classroom. When her impatience led her to glance at a picture and guess at the word rather than take the time to decode it, all I had to do was point to the word to remind her to read it. I did hardly any talking at this stage of her learning. Robin was immensely pleased with herself, as the following excerpts from her record show:

> Robin (5:7) reads all the short-*o* words by transfer without first saying the names of the pictures. Today she also read *job*, *cob*, and *Mom* in a separate booklet. "Now I know how to read *Mom*," she announced proudly. She read *gift* by transfer although she has not yet been taught words ending in a final consonant blend.

Comments:

"I was going to say *fishing pole* because I looked at the picture. But then I read it. It says *rod*."

"I would have said *cow*, but then I read it and I saw it said *ox*."

"I was going to say *pig*, but the word says *hog*."

May 26 (5:8) "I was going to say *bed* but I read it. It says *sick*. I bet he is sick, and he has the mumps, and his cheeks will be like apples."

June 24 (5:9) The following comments show how much she is thinking while she reads:

Reads *socks*: "Why doesn't it have an *x* on the end?"

Reads *beach*: "Why do they have an *a*? I don't hear an /ă/."

Read *because* on her own: "I can read *because*, but I can't write it. That's what's so funny."

Robin's comments show her steadily increasing confidence in her ability to read and transfer her skill to new words. She mastered the reading process by the beginning of first grade and her avid reading kept her ahead. Sometime after Robin went away for the summer—the summer before first grade—I received an exuberant letter from her mother. Robin was going to the library once a week, taking out ten or twelve books at a time and reading them to herself and her younger sister. Needless to say, the parents were thrilled with this reading explosion.

Just as in the case of Bobby, the first question that comes to mind is, Would Robin have learned faster if we had waited until first grade to teach her the letters when she was "more mature?" In this case, the answer came from her first-grade teacher, who called after two months of school to say that she was surprised that Robin could read so fluently. It was puzzling that there was no sign of a perceptual problem in reading, whereas in arithmetic she had great difficulty. She could not learn the symbols. After two months she still reversed numbers and could not keep up with the class. The teacher also wondered why Robin listened attentively to directions whenever writing or reading were concerned, but did not listen to any directions involving arithmetic. I explained that, indeed, Robin had many learning problems—in particular, a poor visual memory. It had taken two lessons a week to teach her how to read. I had not even been able to introduce number symbols.

If simple maturation had been the solution to Robin's problems, she would have learned ten number symbols quickly in first grade. She did not. She needed the same individual help in arithmetic as she had been given in reading.

Bruce is another example of the benefits of an early start. The public school psychologist had found that Bruce's eye-hand coordination was poor: his inability to hold a pencil and follow lines was evident. In all tests requiring sensory-motor coordination, Bruce showed such immaturity that he was considered "not ready" for kindergarten.

The diagnosis was correct. Bruce was not ready. In fact, I had never taught a pupil who literally could not manage to hold a pencil at the age of four-and-a-half. His sense of direction was nil, and his attention span was poor. He refused to draw a line connecting two dots or to write his name. It seemed obvious to me that the gap between his verbal intelligence and his extremely poor motor performance should not be allowed to widen to the extent that he considered himself "hopeless" in that area.

In September we started working together once a week. Bruce needed a lot of additional games to practice tracing, the single most important activity to develop eye-hand coordination. (Tracing is also important in helping to establish the right direction and to prevent reversals.) After five months of hard work, Bruce was able to identify every letter. However, he could not write any of them freehand, and I did not pressure him because it was obvious how inadequate he felt about his lack of ability in that area. Instead, he would dictate to me which letters to write, and then he would trace my letters. Nine months after we had started working together, Bruce volunteered that he would like to write the straight letters on his own. In that lesson he wrote *l*, *f*, and *m*. The magical moment had come—Bruce was "ready" to write letters!

From my own experience I have come to believe that *all* children would benefit from an earlier start. Natural readers, at one end of the continuum, while needing less time to learn, should be taught before they go to school, when their readiness for learning is at a peak. At the other end of the continuum, children like Bobby, Robin, and Bruce, who have some kind of learning problems (which may be affecting the measured IQ), need an earlier, systematic development of the skills necessary for learning to read *successfully*.

Left on their own, they would have reached their critical learning periods too late or never. At six they would not have had the patience or interest to go through the slow learning process of mastering the letters. Through proper teaching, their teachable moment was advanced; they had become interested in letters through playing.

It has been my experience that children with learning difficulties need at least two years to master the reading process. These two years are better spent *before* any formal learning takes place, that is, before first grade, so we can ensure that they do not feel the slightest discouragement.

Even in the best of teaching situations—an open classroom and a warm, supportive teacher—children with learning problems easily feel frustrated. Even if they are allowed to progress at their own rate and follow their own interests, they are no longer interested in learning to identify five or six letters; they are bored. They feel that, being six, they should be able to read, yet here they are struggling with the mastery of only six letters or, worse, unsuccessfully trying to remember the looks of as few as ten words. They feel discouraged about their own performance and thus about themselves, for they do not meet their own standards. Obviously, such negative feelings interfere with the learning they can do.

Given the premise that an early start is desirable for all children, with or without learning problems within the normal IQ range, the question presents itself, Who is going to provide the early start? Ideally, all public school pre-kindergartens and kindergartens should be prepared to teach a structured readiness program to all children. In this way, natural readers could learn to read at their optimum "critical" times, and children with any learning difficulties could have all the learning time they need.

How much these young children learn is unimportant. The point is to give them an enjoyable introduction to the process of learning. Children who have learned the sound names of even six letters will have an easier time in first grade than those who have not begun the learning process.

Learning letters takes time. Previously, preschoolers have not had to concern themselves with direction. They can put together a jigsaw puzzle from top to bottom, from outside to inside, or completely randomly. Children can approach their front doors from several directions and always arrive home. Unlike most other preschool learning, letters (and numbers) go in one definite direction.

Some children take a very long time to develop a sense of direction, but it should be developed—at least to some degree—*before* children learn sound-letter correspondence and before they learn to read.

Some children need additional practice to develop auditory or visual discrimination, or to acquire better eye-hand coordination. Yet if they have not mastered these skills in their preschool period, they will have outgrown an interest in achieving them. For instance, four-year-olds are interested in holding a pencil and being able to write a letter of the alphabet. They are proud of their achievement when they can record a sound they hear by a symbol they have just learned. Six-year-olds are no longer fascinated by such baby stuff. They want to write stories. Yet they, too, have to start at the beginning.

My plea for an early start for *all* children is not made because I feel that they could not learn to read later. It stems from the conviction that children should enter school with a fair chance that they will feel competent from the beginning.

For the past thirty-five years I have tutored four- and five-year-old children who have been diagnosed as having learning disabilities. Those children needed a great deal *more* help with learning sound-letter correspondence than allowed for in kindergarten or in first grade. At the preschool level they had the free time to learn and to develop an interest in learning. Without exception, they experienced success in learning to read.

In contrast, children with identical learning problems who were referred to me *after* they experienced failure had a harder time learning because of the initial blow to their self-esteem. Tragically, they need not have failed and would not have failed if our educational system provided pre-kindergartens and kindergartens that systematically taught reading readiness skills, especially sound-letter knowledge.

Success in school helps establish a positive cycle and, inevitably, brings enjoyment in learning. The satisfaction of achievement is in itself enough to make children want to try hard to learn more. But children who feel inadequate in the beginning of their school lives lose their courage, and their motivation to do well decreases rapidly. Nowadays, young children who meet difficulties are likely to think of themselves as stupid and therefore as failures right from the beginning of their schooling.

The importance of the early years in the development of children's personalities is well known and accepted. Only fairly recently has increasing recognition been given to the importance of the early years in children's cognitive development. Concretely, they must be given stimulation and tools for learning. Psychologically, they must acquire early the feeling of "I can" in the intellectual area. Successful experiences of intellectual competence have a direct influence on children's feelings about themselves, and this is probably the most important single reason for wanting all children to have the chance for an early start in learning to read.

4
Please Don't Teach the ABCs

••

The most important reading readiness skill is the ability to identify letters by their sound names. Children should never be given the job of memorizing the alphabet, which at this stage is simply a meaningless exercise; rather they should be allowed to discover the letters in their natural, intelligible relationship to the sounds heard in words. In this way children learn to use inductive reasoning, an indispensable tool for all future learning.

A whole generation of teachers and parents brought up on the ABC song may well ask, "Why not teach the ABCs? Four-year-olds are so proud when they can recite the ABCs." Knowing the alphabet is an achievement that most children enjoy, but as we shall see, knowing the letter names can be a handicap in learning to read and spell. Whatever the temptation, don't teach the ABCs!

Although preschool children are fascinated by written language, telling them that the letter *m* says /em/ means nothing to them. Modern psychologists such as Piaget have shown that young children can understand a concept only when it is presented on the concrete level. Before learning letters, children must understand that a concrete object such as a mitten has a name and that this name starts with /m/ before they can grasp the idea that the sound /m/ is recorded by the symbol *m*. Only by moving from the concrete to the abstract can children eventually grasp that these strange squiggles on paper, which we call letters, record sounds heard in words they use every day. This genuine insight into the relationship between the concrete and the abstract, between sound and symbol, is crucial. True understanding of symbolic abstractions, in contrast to rote knowledge of the ABCs, represents a gigantic step forward in children's intellectual development, as Jeanne Chall and other educators have pointed out.[1]

---

[1] Jeanne S. Chall, *Learning to Read: The Great Debate* (New York: McGraw-Hill Book Co., 1967), p. 159.

There is another even stronger reason not to teach the ABCs. Personal experience has shown me repeatedly that knowing the alphabet names can be a handicap to children. When reading the word *dog* for the first time, children should be able to sound out the word, /dog/, and realize what it means: "a dog." But they can sound out the word only if they know the sound names of the letters. Merely naming the letters, /dee/ /oh/ /gee/, does not enable them to arrive at the pronunciation /dog/.

Most four- and five-year-olds readily accept the explanation that every letter has two names, a sound name and an alphabet name, which are pronounced differently. For example, when we pronounce the word *fan*, we hear that it starts with an /f/ sound. That is what we call the sound name of the letter; we hear only the pure consonant, not a vowel sound attached to it. The alphabet name /ef/ has a completely different sound. Children readily accept the suggestion that learning the sound names of the letters is what we need when learning to read and spell. They enjoy the idea that letters, just like people, have two names: the sound names are their "first names" and the alphabet names are their "last names." They are amused by the analogy that letters, like children, should be called by their first names and not by their last names.

The Bobby you met in chapter 3 was attending a kindergarten where the alphabet names of the letters were taught. He expressed the difference succinctly, "When I come here, we better never use the last names of the letters. They don't get you to read. When I come here, we better stick to the first names."

Adults are harder to convince of this order of priority. Perhaps they are so accustomed to using only alphabet names that they see this knowledge of the ABCs as more useful than it is. They see the alphabet as a lesson in memorization which, like counting, should simply be taught.

Eric, a remedial student of mine, came across the word *on* in his book. He kept staring at the word and saying /oh/ /en/. But saying /oh/ /en/ did not help him decode this simple word. Systematically, he had to unlearn using the alphabet names of the letters before he could learn to read using a decoding process.

Michael, a second-grade remedial pupil, had been taught only the alphabet names of the letters in school. When he was confronted with a word he didn't know, he said helplessly, "/Double u/ /ee/? /Double u/ /ee/? Which word is it?" Knowing the *sound* name of *w* might well have been a sufficient clue for him to be able to decode the simple word *we*.

Even the mature reader does not use the alphabet names of the letters in reading. Let us assume that you come across a word you do not know in a newspaper. In such a case, would you say to yourself, "/aitch/ /oh/ /em/ /oh/ /tee/ /ay/ /ex/ /eye/ /ess/"? I don't think so. Instead, you sound out the word, "/hō/ /mō/ /tăx/ /ĭs/." Knowledge of the alphabet is needed only for looking up words in a dictionary. That skill, properly introduced in third grade, is facilitated by knowing the sequence of the alphabet.

In contrast, children who know the sound names of the letters and who are given insight into the structure of words possess a basic tool for figuring out a great many words on their own. Examples of this transfer have occurred in many first grades, with children ranging in ability from slow to very bright. These children were able to read words like *has, mad, sad,* and *ran* on their own before they were taught these words.

Knowing the sound names of the letters is equally effective when it comes to spelling. If spelling is taught not through memorization but through analysis and understanding of the structure of words, then knowledge of the alphabet names again proves to be not only wasteful but also detrimental to learning. I have many records of bright first graders who came to me for help knowing only the alphabet names of the letters. When asked to complete *ca* by making the word *cat*, they said /căt/ to themselves, emphasizing the final /t/, as I had shown them, and then looked up and asked, "What shall I write, /cee/, /em/, or /tee/?" The sound /t/ did not automatically make them think of the letter *t*, which they knew only by its alphabet name /tee/.

The roots of spelling, like those of reading, lie in spoken language. Children who have mastered sound-letter correspondence do not need to place an extra burden on their memories by learning to spell by memorizing an unrelated sequence of letters. They know how to spell the word *hat* because they listen to themselves say /h/ /ă/ /t/. They should not be expected to produce an automatic response to the word's alphabet names because they do not *hear* /aitch/ /ay/ /tee/. The word *hat*, furthermore, is a linguistically regular word; they can clearly hear the individual sounds. They can then record these sounds naturally and logically by their letters, *provided they know the sound names of the letters*.

In this instance, it is *adults* who have to unlearn. Adults have to free themselves from the traditional concept that learning to spell requires being able to recite the alphabet names. We should not accept such a narrow definition of spelling. Too many children are taught to spell by memorizing the sequence of letter names: /jay/ /yoo/ /em/ /pee/ spells *jump*. Children who learn to spell this way have to remember the sequence of hundreds of letter names as if they were many different telephone numbers. Children who are taught spelling this way miss out on the exciting discovery that spelling, like reading, has as its base spoken language and is a logical recording of sounds heard in the spoken word.

Thinking ahead to the time when children will be learning other languages, there is another, unexpected advantage to knowing the sound names of the letters: this knowledge provides children with a key not only to learning to read and spell in English but also in many foreign languages. For example, knowing that *f* says /f/ helps them in sounding out not only *father* but also *frère*, *fuente*, and *Frau* in French, Spanish, and German, respectively. Merely knowing that the letter says /ef/ is of no earthly use in learning to read and spell in any language.

Ideally, letters should be taught as recorded *sounds* of spoken words, for speech precedes reading. The sound must be taught first; its transfer to an abstract symbol is a second step.

Discovering the sound names of each letter, which will be discussed in detail in chapter 9, is a learning process that makes sense to children. The first step involves identifying initial sounds. What is the first sound you hear when I say *mitten*? You hear /m/, not /em/. What is the first sound you hear in *fan*? You hear /f/, not /ef/. Only when this skill has been acquired, should the children learn to record a sound they hear by its corresponding letter. If the spoken word *mask* is represented by a picture of a mask with the letter *m* superimposed upon it, children can learn to infer that the letter represents the initial sound of *mask*, which is /m/. Learning letters through deductive reasoning, a form of self-teaching in fact, has more impact than if teachers or parents give the abstractions.

It is, therefore, important to resist the temptation to start the introduction of letters by pointing to a printed letter (or a felt, sandpaper, or magnetic letter) and telling the children the alphabet name of the letter. Instead, begin with spoken words and help children discover that every word they speak has an initial sound. After they can identify *all* the letters by their sound names, and only after this, do you have the option of then teaching the ABCs. Children need these in order to learn the conventional grown-up way of identifying letters, not because the names serve any real function in learning to read and spell. Children who have good inventory memories learn the "last names" of the letters easily, and at that point the alphabet names of the letters do not interfere with reading and spelling.

Some children, however, have poor inventory memories, and they have difficulty learning the correspondence between each letter and its sound name. Some children, like Bobby, mentioned in chapter 3, have difficulty with intrasensory transfer. It is hard for them to hear /m/, then point to the visual form *m*. These children should not be introduced to a second auditory form of each letter, especially since they still have to learn a second visual form of each letter (the capital) to be able to read sentences and proper names. It is essential that children with any of these learning difficulties not be burdened with learning the alphabet names of the letters at a time when such knowledge is ornamental rather than functional. In these cases it is always advisable to postpone the teaching of the ABCs.

When should these children who have poor inventory memories learn the traditional alphabet? Children who learn to read systematically through decoding only linguistically regular words like *cat, pin*, and *mop* need to learn the alphabet names of the vowels before they come to the decoding of words like *cane* or *pine*, in which we use the alphabet names of the vowels in reading. They do not need to know the alphabet names of the consonants. Sometime, perhaps not until third grade, when they can read and write fluently, they can be taught the alphabet names of the letters both as a means of communication (no child wants to go through life referring to the letter *m* as /m/) and to aid in acquiring dictionary skills.

How to Help Children Spell

Even if children know the alphabet names of the letters, don't ask them to spell words orally. Have them write the words. In this way they are spared countless hours of memorizing spelling words—a lifesaver for all those children who may be bright but who have poor memories. Even an irregular word has some relation to spoken language; for instance, the word *night* has a correspondence between sounds and letters at beginning and end. Children need only to remember that the silent *gh* in the middle makes the preceding vowel long. This is easier to learn than to commit the entire word, letter by letter, to memory (see chapter 10).

HOW TO HELP CHILDREN WRITE THEIR NAMES

As a teacher I have come across countless children, some as young as three, who print their names in capital letters. In fact, capital letters are taught in most kindergartens on the ground that capitals are easier to print than lowercase letters because all are the same height, whereas lowercase letters vary in size. But many children who have learned to write their names in capitals while they are in kindergarten find it incredibly difficult to break this habit in first grade, as any first-grade teacher will testify.

So if children ask you to write their names for them, give them a model starting with a capital and the rest of the name printed in lowercase letters, for example, *Bobby*. First let the children trace your model with their fingers. Show them where to start. Watch them. You don't want to take the chance that on their own they might trace their names backward; such a habit is hard to break. Now let them go over their names with a crayon or pencil. Unobtrusively dot their names on all of their drawings or collages and have them trace your model.

TEACHING CHILDREN LOWERCASE LETTERS

In chapter 9 you will find out how to teach four-year-old children to trace and later to write letters. You will be teaching them lowercase letters only. Why? We do not use capital letters in writing except at the beginning of a proper name or the beginning of the first word in a sentence. Thus the letters children write most often will be lowercase.

One of my present students, Mia (6:5), goes to a kindergarten where the teacher insists on teaching the pupils capital letters and lowercase letters simultaneously. By now, Mia has learned both forms, but she cannot remember which is which. Figure 4.1 illustrates her confusion.

In Mia's case, I can help her overlearn the lowercase letters, especially since she will soon stop kindergarten for the summer. And since she enjoys all the tracing games, she doesn't even realize she is practicing lowercase letters.

But from third grade on, and especially in high school, students who make similar mistakes, such as writing *THeRe, MAn,* or *floWeR,* will not participate in tracing or writing games. It's too late. They

Figure 4.1 Page from Mia's workbook (Book B)

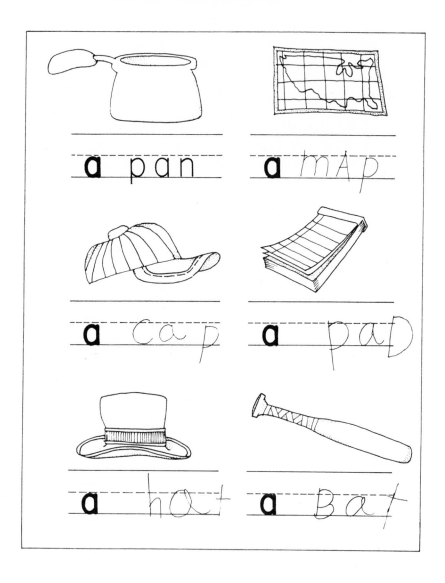

only want to catch up with their classmates; they have neither the interest nor the time to learn how to write properly.

By being introduced to only lowercase letters at first, children have an opportunity to practice them as much as they need to through tracing games. These games not only help children form these letters, but also help with the more difficult task of aligning them. It would be helpful if alphabet books, games, and educational television programs such as the otherwise excellent "Sesame Street" would teach only the lowercase forms of the letters and the sound names of the letters.

The arguments against teaching capital letters before lowercase letters and against using the ABCs will make sense to you if you realize that as an adult, you do not usually write words in capital letters. Nor do you make use of the ABCs in reading. So why teach them to children who are just venturing into reading and writing? It will only conflict with their learning.

5
When Parents Can Teach and When They Cannot
···

Please, choose carefully whom to ask for the answer to the question implied by the title of this chapter. There are very persuasive, well-meaning experts in the area of early childhood education who hold to the conventional wisdom that a *teacher, not a parent*[1] should develop children's reading readiness skills and that only a first-grade teacher can teach children reading. Furthermore, these experts will admonish you that children are not ready to learn to read until they are at least six years old.

What a dilemma! If you wait and leave the actual teaching to the school, will your children, in a perhaps overcrowded class, run the risk of never learning to read, or at best, never enjoying it? Yet if you go ahead and teach your preschoolers to read, will you be interfering with their natural, healthy development and possibly cause worse damage? As in so many other areas of child-rearing, you parents probably often feel you are damned if you do and damned if you don't!

In answering the argument that early teaching might interfere with the children's "natural, healthy development and possibly cause damage" I refer you to Jeanne S. Chall, who writes, "Doesn't an *early* (italics mine) knowledge of, or an interest in, letters mark a new step in the child's intellectual development? The alphabet is a code, an abstraction, perhaps the first that the child learns. Pointing to and naming a letter, or writing a letter, at an early age is quite different from pointing to or drawing a picture of a cat, truck, or a tree. The child who can identify or reproduce a letter engages in symbolic representation, while the child who is working with the picture of an actual object engages in iconic representation. When the child en-

[1] Originally, I wrote this chapter for parents only, but in today's society in which both parents often have to work, a good childcare provider can follow the suggestions in this book.

gages in symbolic representation, he is already practicing a higher form of intellectual behavior."[2]

The above quotation presents the strongest argument why you are *not* interfering with your preschoolers' natural development when you teach them sound-letter knowledge and early reading skills. Actually, you are helping your children to a new step "in their intellectual development," a step so exciting to children that it will ensure their continued motivation to learn.

After many years of consulting and teaching experience, I consider age four (occasionally four and a half, but never before four) as an optimum age to start developing sound-letter knowledge. By this age, children have a good command of the spoken language, the crucial basis on which mastery of the written language rests. In addition, they usually have adequate gross muscular coordination, a prerequisite for the development of eye-hand coordination.

Starting at four gives children *two years* to learn all the readiness skills and sound-letter correspondence. Learning to identify letters is a difficult process, and one that takes a great deal more time and practice than is allowed for in first grade.

In all their previous experiences, preschoolers learned that an object is constant no matter which direction it faces. John Money termed this phenomenon "object constancy."[3] When young children correctly identify a table or a chair even though it is lying upside down, or when they can recognize "tableness" or "chairness" despite a shape or perspective that is new to them, we think they are highly intelligent. But when later they identify a *w* as an *m* or a *u* as an *n*, they are wrong even though the shape is so similar.

A teddy bear is a teddy bear no matter which way it looks. A dog is still a dog whether it faces to the left or the right. This is not true in the world of symbols in which direction becomes crucial. When children learn to identify or write letters, they now have to obey the law of "directional constancy" (John Money). Thus when a *d* faces to the right it becomes a *b*. Or when a *p* faces to the left it may become a *g* or a *q*.

An added difficulty is the fact that the differences between letters are often minute, whereas the differences between toys or objects

[2]Jeanne S. Chall, *Learning to Read: The Great Debate* (New York: McGraw-Hill Book Co., 1967), p. 159.

[3]John Money, ed., *On Learning and Not Learning to Read*, a chapter in *The Disabled Reader, Education of the Dyslexic Child* (Baltimore: The Johns Hopkins Press, 1966), p. 21.

are easily perceived. For instance, the letters *f*, *l*, and *t* look alike to many children who need a great deal of tracing practice before they can identify each of these letters.

Some of my preschool pupils, admittedly with severe visual perceptual difficulties, needed six weeks to learn to distinguish the letter *m* from the letter *f*. Some of them had only mastered six letters when they went to kindergarten, yet none of my preschoolers ever made a remark that might indicate feelings of frustration or failure.

Unfortunately, most six-year-olds need just as much time and practice as four-year-olds. Just being older does not make for faster learning. In addition, six-year-olds face a huge stumbling block: they cannot possibly have as much time as they need to learn letters. The first grade teacher is under pressure to teach all the letters (or worse: fifty words as sight vocabulary) within the first two months of first grade.

In addition, six-year-olds, who are so much more sophisticated than four-year-olds, come to first grade expecting to learn how to read. They have been able to understand quite intricate stories on tv; now they want to learn to read books. Learning to identify letters seems a very pedestrian, if not boring task. The critical period has passed.

First graders watching their peers learning how to read while they are still struggling with a few letters quickly feel discouraged. Their self-esteem goes downhill. Nothing spirals downward faster than a sense of failure! Most first graders, referred to me by the end of first grade, confided to me, "I am no good at this. I'm stupid. All my friends learned faster." Comments like these are not isolated instances; rather they appear in most of my records.

In contrast, four-year-olds have boundless time to learn; at this age they have no peers to compete against. Furthermore, they are genuinely interested in what the letters say, and they are at the perfect age to enjoy games with an adult. Their interest in the play aspect prevents them from keeping track of how many letters they have mastered; in fact, they feel proud when they have learned only two letters.

Preschool children make no distinction between learning and playing, at least not until they go to school. So another advantage in helping children to read when they want to learn is that they will regard it as play.

There are a few specific reasons why teaching your preschool children should be successful. Your children will enjoy the individual attention, especially in a family where it is not always easy to come by. Children who get restless when you are on the phone, or when you hold a discussion with another grown-up, are delighted to have you to themselves during their special play time.

Parents who have enjoyed playing simple games with their children will find that using readiness games is much the same and equally enjoyable. What it takes is patience and a relaxed feeling of the immediate goals to be achieved, and, above all, a sense of sheer fun.

You can only accomplish this if you feel unpressured and can concentrate on establishing a relaxed setting where you will use the games as described in the following chapters. Your goal is to keep the children's natural curiosity in reading and writing alive—not how much or how fast they can learn.

There are families in which purposeful games can provide yet another advantage. Game time can give a rebellious youngster a new, successful medium of exchange with parents that transcend the old pattern. Suppose, for example, that a three-and-a-half-year-old is jealous of a new baby in the home. His anger surfaces by his saying "no" to everything. What the child really wants is more of his parents' undivided attention. By playing readiness games with this troubled child or by reading to him, the parent could give him a sense of an enjoyable new status.

It is not always a new baby who arouses jealousy; it may well be a younger sibling who, because of his age, requires more help and attention from the parent, and thus makes the older child feel angry and rejected. Having her special time with the parent by playing reading readiness games which, after all, are too difficult for the younger brother, convinces the older child that there are many advantages to being older.[4]

Incidentally, fathers are sometimes more effective teachers than mothers, simply because their patience may be less eroded by domestic concerns. Fathers and mothers alike enjoy playing with their children, and many welcome a concrete plan of action such as a session of readiness games as a pleasant way of spending time with their children.

Many parents have found it helpful to set aside a definite time for reading games. Such an arrangement, however loose, lends struc-

---

[4]If distractions from the younger sibling are too great, you might want to hire a babysitter for an hour and set that time aside for your child and yourself.

ture to the play time. Also, *time* for reading games might evaporate if not built into the busy family schedule. As a personal aside, I taught my own children when they were around four; I set aside a half hour immediately after supper for their play time with me. From the beginning, it was impossible for me to get out of this commitment, even though I would have liked sometimes to tackle the dishes first.

I taught my oldest granddaughter, Gabriela, when she was four years old, every day after breakfast. Once she could read the ŏ-words, she would bounce into my room around 8 P.M. asking, "May I have another lesson now?" At eleven, she reads everything and everywhere. I noticed that her father had to take her book away from her on the bus, because it had gotten very dark.

Gabriela's younger sister, Monica, lived with her family in Nicaragua when she was four. When she came back and I arrived for visits, Monica, too, appeared for her lesson after breakfast. But Monica wanted a new game for every lesson, so I owe many games in this book to Monica and other inquisitive students.

I "taught" my youngest granddaughter, Hallie, for the first time two days before her third birthday; we played games from chapter seven. Each time, Hallie insisted that she have a turn asking me what she took away, for instance. After four games, I stopped: I didn't want to risk the magic disappearing.

From personal experience, I can recommend that these games are ideally suited for grandparents. No advance shopping, and you can sit and rest while enjoying your grandchildren's fun!

One important point: you may have children who, while very cooperative and obviously enjoying the games, may have mastered only ten to twelve letters when entering first grade. Don't be discouraged! Your children will have understood far more than just ten letters; they will have grasped the learning process that letters record sounds and that they must go in a prescribed direction, an insight that will speed up their future learning. You have helped them acquire a good foundation on which to develop early reading skills.

But once your children enter first grade, you cannot continue teaching them at home. At this point, home teaching can interfere with their progress at school. The lines of authority must be clear. If they are not, children may become confused and conclude that the parents have no faith in the teacher. Obviously, an occasional game does not do any harm.

Don't give up helping your child in other areas concerning school work. For instance, it is important that you express interest in your children's work and help them develop good work habits by setting aside a definite time and a quiet place to do their homework. Your pride and excitement in your children's intellectual progress is very important in spurring them on to more learning.

At the other end of the spectrum, you will have children who can read words and sentences on their own when they enter kindergarten. They are jubilant, and children share each discovery with their parents. A new, almost magic bond develops between parent and children, for it is you, the parent, who has given your children the magic key to this enchanted land where they can discover reading!

There are, however, family situations when neither parent should teach their own children almost from the very beginning. As always, there are no hard and fast rules here. If you are not a patient person, if your expectations are too high, and you worry when your children take too long to catch on, you may not be able to teach them. Your impatience will communicate itself and thus defeat the purpose.

Such parents may also persist after children have lost interest. Rigidity of any kind either by insisting on certain games or holding on to game time when youngsters have made plans with friends, can have unhappy results in terms of children's spontaneous interest in learning.

There may be periods in your life when you cannot give your undivided attention to your child in these readiness sessions. Then it is probably better not to attempt them at all. Children are quick to sense when an adult's attention is elsewhere, and this can cause real resistance.

In some families there is an obvious clash of temperaments between parents and children—sometimes because they are so similar. If this is true of you and your children, you should not teach them. The chances are, you will never be comfortable together in a game situation.

But don't think that difficulties in a teaching situation are always due to the parent. There are children who, for any number of reasons, feel compelled to fight their parents every step of the way. Without guilt or defeatism, we must accept the fact that our children, like everyone else, are different: some seem to have more difficult temperaments than others and are harder to raise. Second or third children often seem easier to bring up, simply because they have never been displaced. Also we are more experienced and therefore more relaxed as parents.

If your children are fighters, asserting themselves stubbornly and negatively at any suggestion from you, however subtly it may be, you may have difficulty getting them to play games or even to listen to a story. Rather than letting conflicts occur, stop immediately and bow out gracefully. Even if you have to let the teaching go for a month, or finally find a good substitute, never risk a confrontation. You will never win—simply because you are their parents. It is possible that their resistance toward the games, for instance, is really directed toward your authority. By forcing your children to learn, you are taking the chance that they will transfer their negativism from you to the act of reading. Once they are set against reading, that negativism is very difficult to change.

GETTING OUTSIDE HELP FOR NATURAL READERS

If, for whatever reason, you have decided that you cannot teach your own preschool children, don't give up. If your children are natural readers, and want to be taught (but not by you!) make the effort to find outside help to teach them.

There are a number of alternatives, if you decide that you cannot teach your own children. Good preschools, if they include in their program a short but definite time for the development of structured readiness activities, are very effective. Modified Montessori preschools (called American Montessori Schools) are ideal, because they include in their program creative activities as well as individual instruction in letters and numbers.[5]

Maria Montessori, while working with retarded children from the slums of Rome at the turn of the century, came to the conclusion that young children enjoy learning to read, write, and do arithmetic in the same way as they enjoy creative activities. Her conviction was that many children, free to choose, prefer work to play, because they enjoy the challenge of a purposeful, structured task. She believed that young children's sensitive periods for learning letters occur early, at four or five, that at that time, their desire and curiosity are at a peak, and consequently, they thrive in a learning environment structured for their needs. In a Montessori school, many learning materials are displayed on open shelves: children can choose which games to play

---

[5]In contrast, International Montessori Schools adhere to the original theory of Maria Montessori which, because children love to learn, banned all creative play from the curriculum. It is tragic that Montessori insisted that all her followers should stick to her rigid theory.

and ask the teacher to help them with any new game that may well involve learning letters or numbers.

Good kindergartens that have a readiness program which includes sound-letter knowledge are also an excellent solution. If your children are natural readers they will thrive there.

If there is no suitable preschool or kindergarten available to you, your next decision depends on what outside help is available. If you are lucky enough to have an extended family living close by, you might call on a grandparent, aunt, or uncle who would enjoy playing games with your children and watching them learn.

You might consider hiring an interested high school student. Most preschool children take to this particular age group and enjoy attention from teenagers. Your local high school principal (write for an appointment) is a good person to look to for help in choosing someone for this job. Naturally, you will pick a warm person who likes children and who has the necessary patience to teach them.

Arrange a time with the student when the two of you can go over the directions for playing the games involved in developing reading readiness before he or she begins teaching your child. The student should know that each picture must be identified correctly in all of the games, and that the child is to be taught a letter as recording the initial sound of a meaningful, spoken word. Points to be emphasized are that the sound names of the letters, not the alphabet names, are to be used, and that the games are self-corrective. If the child makes a mistake, the teacher does not have to say "wrong!" but simply point to the correct letter picture.

If your child has learned all the letters and wants to learn to read, you need to take time out and explain the learning-to-read process to the young teacher. The teacher must understand that teaching someone to read does not consist of telling the pupil what a word or sentence says in a book. Instead, the teacher should follow the method set forth in this book, using linguistically regular words only. By using the games, she/he will understand that the initial reading instruction is a learning process that a child can understand and use as a tool. It is *not* a series of words to be memorized.

Once teacher and pupil have experienced the excitement that comes from independent decoding, neither of them will need your guidance. Leave them alone and judge the success of the experiment by your child's reaction. As long as she continues to like having the student come to the house, you are safe. Don't ask her to evaluate her teacher, but confine your supervision to direct discussion with the teacher later. Be willing to give this teenager time and understand that she/he, too, needs your approval and praise.

If your child is ready for first grade and has been receiving help from an outsider, I suggest a conference with the tutor, the first-grade teacher, and yourself to decide whether the outside teaching can be discontinued. In my own practice, I tried to finish tutoring preschool children by the time they entered first grade. Should this not be possible, let the tutor continue, but in close cooperation with the first-grade teacher. An outside tutor belongs to the "school system" in the eyes of a child, as well as those of a teacher.

GETTING OUTSIDE HELP FOR CHILDREN WITH LEARNING DISABILITIES

Children with learning disabilities need more time to learn than natural readers. They should have that time when they are interested in letters, enjoy playing games, and before they develop the fear that they are not as good as their peers. Early intervention not only prevents their learning disabilities from escalating, but increases their motivation to learn.

You should not teach your own children even if they have just a few of the learning disabilities similar to the ones described in this book. None of the children whose records are presented in chapters three and twelve could have been taught by their parents. In each case there was a different constellation of factors, but one factor was consistent: the children lacked some, if not all, of the readiness skills required to learn to read. Hence the initial learning was hard, and all the children felt easily frustrated.

Parents cannot possibly have the detachment or patience to ride with the frustrations and setbacks that inevitably occur. Nor do they have the specialized training usually required to teach children with serious learning disabilities.

In these cases it takes objective outsiders (usually, but not always, professionals) who have the detachment and trained skills to help these children over the initial hurdles. They can judge the proper balance between modifying the task, so the children will finally meet success, and encouraging them enough, so that they will keep on trying. Children who are frustrated by the lack of aptitude in a given area may take this out on a parent by digging in their heels, whereas they would continue the game with a teacher with whom they have a different, less loaded relationship.

There are several possibilities if you can't teach your preschool children. Again, an enriched American Montessori preschool can be ideal, especially one with special classes for children with learning disabilities.

Or, if your child is five and you think you live near a good public school kindergarten consisting of small classes, find out if it offers a structured readiness program which includes sound-letter correspondence. Arrange for a conference with the kindergarten teacher early in the year to find out how your child is getting along. If she/he is having difficulty keeping up with the class, I suggest getting an outside tutor. You may want to look for a high school student as was discussed earlier in this chapter. In one such instance I found a student willing to work during the summer with a child who was to attend public school kindergarten in the fall. I had suggested half-an-hour every morning as a suitable beginning; after two weeks the child insisted on playing games for one hour.

If you need an adult for the job, look for a warm and accepting graduate student or a teacher on leave of absence. Aside from liking children, she or he must be convinced that teaching sound-letter correspondence before children go to school will pay dividends in first grade. She or he must be willing to teach children with games, as outlined in this book, and understand the importance of allowing children to learn at their own pace.

Should your child experience difficulties in learning, even with a private tutor, I suggest you have your child's learning disabilities diagnosed by a psychologist, or a learning disabilities or reading specialist. If the expert's evaluation shows that your child has many specific learning disabilities, I recommend that your child be tutored by a reading specialist to ensure that your child doesn't experience failure upon entering first grade. It makes sense to tutor preschool children, for it takes *less* time and *less* effort (and *less* money) to prevent the damage that is later so difficult to undo.

The majority of your extended family, friends, and neighbors will, in all probability, bombard you with arguments against having your four-year-old tutored. The most well-meaning friends always advise, "Wait. Your child is so young." Ask them if they would recommend waiting if your four-year-old has a bad toothache or bad stomach pains. In the former case you would most certainly be advised to take your child to a dentist. In the latter case, you'd be urged to take your child to a doctor immediately just in case the pains indicate the necessity of an appendectomy. To me, tutoring a four-year-old is just as urgent. It is wise to do something *before* the small cavity becomes huge and unbearably painful. Parents certainly have persistent stomach aches checked rather than running the risk of having their child undergo an appendectomy.

In summary, in developing reading readiness skills it is crucial that you, the parents, are convinced that teaching at the critical period in your child's life is the all important issue. Starting your children *before* four is risky, because the children's understanding is not mature enough for understanding the connection between sound and symbol. But waiting until *after* four is equally risky. You will probably miss the critical period when your children have the most interest in learning, and, not insignificantly, the most time for it.

It is, of course, most unusual to quote Shakespeare in connection with developing reading readiness skills. But extracting the meaning only and not its literal content or its dire prophecy, the following quotation fits:

> There is a tide in the affairs of men,
> Which, taken at the flood, leads on to fortune;
> Omitted, all the voyage of their life
> Is bound in shallows and in miseries.[6]

---

[6]William Shakespeare, *Julius Caesar,* Act IV, Scene III. (New York: Avenel Books) 1975.

6
Building Foundations: Toys, Play, and Reading Aloud

··

Babies start to learn from birth, and you as parents play an important part in these early learning experiences. The importance of the parents' role cannot be overemphasized. Dolores Durkin,[1] in her research study conducted in New York City in 1965, concluded that the difference between early readers and nonreaders lies not so much in the children, but in the parents. The parents of nonreaders usually have little or no time for their children and, interestingly, are much more willing to accept the school's suggestion that they leave the teaching of reading and writing to the school. Dolores Durkin's research emphasizes that parents of early readers generally enjoy playing with their children. They find the time to talk to them, to answer and ask questions, and to read to them.

You can help your children build a secure foundation for reading by actively enriching their early years and by being sensitive and attuned to their critical periods of interest and capability. Even in your babies' first months, you influence their ability to learn. By fostering their curiosity and the acuteness of their five senses, you are providing your babies with the first stepping stones to learning. The time you give and the games you play develop your babies' readiness for learning.

You can provide materials and toys to stimulate your babies. For instance, babies learning to focus their eyes will be interested in the slight movement of mobiles attached to their cribs. They learn to follow moving objects with their eyes. Or they enjoy holding a small ball or rattle and moving it themselves while they are being dressed. This is the very beginning of the development of concentration, essential to all learning.

Toddlers learning to walk are soon running in all directions.

---

[1]Dolores Durkin, *Children Who Read Early: Two Longitudinal Studies* (New York: Teachers College Press, 1966), pp. 94–96.

"They are into everything," the weary parent or teacher complains. But in the course of their active explorations, most toddlers will voluntarily sit down and "work" hard at some object they have discovered. Having found your pots and pans, they may try very hard to fit a lid on a pot. Or while taking apart your percolator, and possibly trying to put it back together again, their faces express deep concentration. Respect the appearance of that concentration because its development is one of the most important steps in preparing children for learning. From their earliest years, encourage them to develop and extend their natural periods of concentration and involvement. Don't interrupt. Understand the importance of their absorption even if they take the percolator apart.

EDUCATIONAL TOYS AND ACTIVITIES FOR THE TWO- TO THREE-YEAR-OLD

At this age, children need some educational toys: toys that have a built-in task to be solved, such as arranging brightly colored rings in order from the smallest to the largest. Mariann Winick, in her book *Before the 3 R's*,[2] gives innumerable suggestions about making educational games for very little cost.

Commercial toys should have an educational function, a task that children can understand and solve—for instance, a box with cut-out geometric slots so that a circle will fit only into a circular hole. A simple jigsaw puzzle with just a few pieces is very useful, especially if an adult works it with them. However, as explained in chapters 4 and 9, children shouldn't be given magnetic letters or toys bearing the alphabet with the idea of teaching them their names.

Try to restrict the number of toys. Too many interfere with concentration. A favorite object or two, a good educational toy, and a puzzle should be within reach at any given time so children have the chance to work and play without too much disorganization. This way they can enjoy the absorption of a task and then the feeling of success at having completed it. Success generates success. The satisfaction of "It fits! I have done it!" will spur them on to further efforts.

Be sure not to overlook the importance of such large muscle activities as catching or rolling a large ball, balancing on a line or crack without slipping off, and learning to skip and to use playground

[2]Mariann P. Winick, *Before the 3 R's* (New York: David McKay Company, 1973).

equipment. Finding ways for children to practice these activities to develop gross motor coordination is essential for subsequently learning to read. Gross motor coordination precedes the development of eye-hand coordination, which is the next necessary step.

When you observe youngsters trying to place pegs in holes or making their first scribbles, be sure they have crayons, paper, blunt kindergarten scissors, and old magazines at their disposal. Cutting out pictures and making "drawings" develop eye-hand coordination. What is important is that they are holding a crayon and using both eyes and hands to guide it. The drawing that is produced is immaterial. Young children are sometimes eager to start "writing," but don't encourage this because they may teach themselves letters incorrectly, and as discussed in chapters 4 and 9, the only learning sequence that allows for discovery involves sounds first and letters later. Teachers and parents can encourage the development of children's eye-hand coordination by showing them a particular skill or activity a few times and then letting them practice on their own. For instance, let them struggle with their socks even though it may take a lot longer than if the parent helped them, or let them feed themselves in spite of the inevitable mess. Here, too, the feelings of achievement and competence eventually contribute to the formal learning process.

LETTING CHILDREN HELP AROUND THE HOUSE AND CLASSROOM

Even young children enjoy helping around the house. It makes them feel independent to be able to put their cups and saucers (unbreakable, I suggest) in the sink. Climbing on a chair to reach the sink will develop their motor coordination, and their self-esteem will be bolstered by being considered old enough to help.

Similarly, children in a preschool or day care center should be encouraged to put on their own clothes and to help with simple jobs in the classroom. If children make a mess, ignore it. Don't measure their jobs against any standards, but thank them for their helpfulness. What matters is that you allow them to sense their growing competence through independence.

Both at home or in preschool or day care, talk to the children about the jobs they are doing for you. By asking and answering questions, children will develop their speech and their comprehension.

DEVELOPING LANGUAGE

Once children have become physiologically mature enough to talk, the response and encouragement of the people around them makes an enormous difference in how fast and accurately they learn to express themselves. If teachers and parents show delight at every new word or sentence children say, they will encourage them to develop oral language skills at their own rate.

Pronounce clearly the name of each object children point to; they will soon copy you. Don't correct their sentence structure or pronunciation when they are trying to tell you something important; their first need is communication, not correction. Do it later, if necessary, perhaps in the form of a game. Always speak to them distinctly and carefully and in complete sentences. You are their model, and they'll copy your ways of talking.

At the same time that children are expanding their vocabularies, let them learn new concepts from you. Help them to identify colors or to use numbers (on a spoken, concrete level) or to name objects in categories, such as food, toys, or clothes. This ability to classify is a prerequisite for learning to read.

ENLARGING THE WORLD OF CHILDREN

Trips and even small excursions are important ways of enlarging children's experiences. Take children to the supermarket, zoo, aquarium, subway, or airport. As early as eighteen months children will enjoy these outings. Talk to them as you venture forth. Your observations about these new places help to enrich their speaking vocabularies. More questions from the children indicate that they are ready for more answers; they become familiar with and verbal about places they may meet later in books. The more direct verbal interchanges children have, as Dr. Burton L. White, director of Harvard's Pre-School Project, points out, "the better off they are in comparison to watching and listening to television."[3]

TELEVISION AND EARLY LEARNING

At this point, something has to be said about television. There is no doubt that television helps children by enriching their speaking vocabularies, particularly those whose families are not able to do so.

[3]Burton L. White, *The First Three Years of Life* (Englewood, N.J.: Prentice-Hall, Inc., 1975), p. 160.

But television will never be a substitute for live interaction, and on the whole, it makes for passive listeners. Selected good television programs such as "Sesame Street" and "The Electric Company" or shows about animals are outstanding exceptions; yet even watching the good programs must be supervised judiciously so that children do not become passively glued to the set.

Some parents might say, "Look how well these children learn to concentrate. They sit for hours watching tv." This kind of acvivity does not count as mental effort and concentration. Such children are not really thinking; they are just sitting.

Using television to enrich rather than to stultify is one of the most difficult tasks that parents have. From the very beginning, parents rather than children must be in control of the television. Children must get used to the idea that two or three favorite programs is all they are allowed, no matter how big a temper tantrum they can throw. The television must not be used as a babysitter.

Within these limits, parents have the option of ameliorating the bad effects of television. They can watch a good program with their children. Together they might enjoy a show about wild animals. Parents or teachers should ask and answer questions about specific happenings, thus sharpening children's observations. In this way, watching television becomes a shared experience, one that imperceptibly requires more active watching on the part of the children. If you are present when children pick up a word or an idea from television without really knowing what it means, you can talk it over with them. This helps them learn what the terminology or concept means.

Watching television together, however, can never be a substitute for reading to children or playing games with them, both of which lengthen their attention spans and develop their abilities to concentrate.

READING ALOUD TO CHILDREN

Looking at books and being read to are two of the best preparations for learning to read to oneself. Toddlers who sit down with a book on their own may do so because they are imitating their older siblings and parents, but they may also become genuinely fascinated. In the beginning it is better to choose reality-oriented books rather than fantasy books: picture books with simple, uncluttered illustrations of objects or animals to identify, such as *Goodnight Moon*[4] and *The Snowy Day*.[5] Then a simple story like *Have You Seen My Cat?*[6] takes the step from identifying pictures to identifying situations. And the children can learn to turn the pages by themselves.

Sitting close to a teacher or a parent at reading time enables children to absorb through a kind of psychological osmosis the adult's understanding, humor, and warmth. Children will catch the adults' love of books, their enjoyment of a good story, and their appreciation of good illustrations. Last but by no means least, children will cherish the special bond that grows from sharing books with an adult.

Children who are used to regular or frequent reading will be ready to progress from picture books to nursery rhymes and story books between the ages of two and three. As they grow older, the books to be read aloud can become more difficult to keep up with the children's rapidly developing understanding of the world around them. Books for reading aloud can be ahead of the children's chronological age and often ahead of the recommended age set by librarians, which is usually based on the children's ability to read to themselves. Adults can, therefore, introduce books that would be much too hard were the children to try to read them to themselves.

How you read is important. Emphasizing important words will help children understand the sequence of the story. A warm tone of voice indicates your interest, whereas a patronizing tone may alienate the children. Your way of reading may well become the model of how the children themselves will later read. If you yourself are really paying attention to what is happening in *The Story of Babar*[7] or *Madeline*[8] or *Sam Who Never Forgets*,[9] the children's imaginations and their senses of humor will also catch fire. Also their feelings for animals and people in the story, their understanding of themselves, and their relation to others will grow.

Children naturally thrive on an adult's warm attention during the story time spent together. Speaking vocabularies are enlarged as children make the connection between words and pictures. Children get

---

[4]Margaret Wise Brown, *Goodnight Moon* (New York: Harper & Row, reprint, 1975).

[5]Ezra Jack Keats, *The Snowy Day* (New York: Viking Press, 1960).

[6]Eric Carle, *Have You Seen My Cat?* (Jacksonville, MA: Picture Book Studio, 1987).

[7]Jean DeBrunhoff, *The Story of Babar* (New York: Random House, 1933).

[8]Ludwig Bemelmans, *Madeline* (New York: Viking Press, 1967).

[9]Eve Rice, *Sam Who Never Forgets* (New York: Mulberry Books, 1977).

used to sitting quietly and paying attention. Soon the adult can make simple suggestions: "Show me the horse. Show me the cow." Later the adult can ask questions: "Who found the ball? Where did they live? What did you see when you went to the zoo?"

As children get older, ask more difficult questions that will teach them to interpret the story. Get them to identify the main character, to describe the sequence of events, or to determine cause and effect. Occasionally, children may like to make up their own ending to the story. By responding to questions, children will develop their imaginations and reasoning abilities.

All of these comprehension skills must be developed and practiced before children are able to use these skills in written language. This preparation is essential. Just as speech precedes reading, full use and comprehension of *spoken* language must precede that of *written* language.

Some young children who are being read to point to certain words in the book, asking "Does this word say 'Babar'?" or "Which word says 'Daddy'?" Some children, at a very early age, pick out certain letters whose shapes and patterns they like and are delighted with their ability to recognize these letters whenever they occur. While these children should be given the proper answer—the name of the word and the sound name of the letter (not its alphabet name!)—I would not interpret these questions to be a signal to teach them reading. Three (or two) is not the optimum time for teaching youngsters reading. As has been said, they are too young to grasp symbolic abstractions.

The age of three is, however, the best time for developing specific readiness skills. Enlarging the speaking vocabulary and gaining facility in using language, both as a means of communication and as a way of expressing thoughts, are the important gains for this age and must precede learning printed symbols. Three-year-old children have many questions to ask, and the adult's job is to answer them precisely. Today's children are smarter earlier than former generations were because of the increased complexity and stimulation of the world around them. But the ability to actively absorb, organize, and understand what they have perceived requires the help of the grown-up.

7
Readiness Games for Three-year-olds

Playing games offers a unique opportunity to help children develop many specific readiness skills essential for their success in learning to read. While the readiness skills do not follow a strict one, two, three order, there is a general sequence in children's abilities to master them, and the adult should follow it. For instance, children *first* have to learn to identify objects or pictures by their proper names and to observe details in a picture. Only *after* they have learned these skills are they able to understand what *sequence* or *classifying* means.

Following is an overview of all the readiness skills, divided for the sake of convenience according to age groups. This particular breakdown shows that each major building block rests on the completion of the preceding one and does not suggest the exact age at which children should start to develop certain skills.

Three-year-olds should be encouraged to develop their abilities:

- to listen
- to expand their speaking vocabularies
- to concentrate
- to observe, e.g., to select a given object in a picture
- to follow directions
- to develop eye-hand coordination, e.g., to guide a pencil
- to follow a prescribed direction, learning left-to-right progression

Three-and-a-half- to four-year-olds (see chapter 8) should be encouraged to develop their abilities:

- to understand sequence
- to classify
- to develop fine auditory discrimination, specifically, to identify initial sounds of spoken words

Four- to four-and-a-half-year-olds (see chapter 9) should be encouraged to develop their abilities:

- to understand sound-letter correspondence
- to develop fine visual discrimination, specifically, to identify letters

SKILLS FOR THREE-YEAR-OLDS

Let us see what the skills for three-year-olds involve:

❏ Listening

Toddlers have started to develop this ability by sitting down to listen to you. Children who learn to enjoy listening to a story are prepared well for "listening" to an author tell a story, i.e., for reading.

❏ Expanding Speaking Vocabularies

Speech precedes writing. Children have to know what a lemon *is* or what a tiger *is*, to give but two examples, before they can understand the written counterparts. Children who have a good command of spoken language, who are encouraged to learn new terms and concepts, will comprehend their meaning in print.

❏ Concentrating

Children who are capable of focusing on a task, of shutting out all distracting stimuli, are prepared for all learning, not just reading.

Learning to concentrate, listed here as one of the readiness skills, is basic to *all* learning. Playing any one of the games described later in this chapter helps children to learn to focus on a task. Today, quite a few children are labeled as having an "attentional deficit order." No doubt many of these have a neurological basis for this disorder, but in some cases, this behavioral deficit occurred because early on concentration was not developed.

❏ Observing—Selecting a Given Object in a Picture

This readiness skill is a prerequisite for the development of finer visual discrimination, which is required in the identification of letters. Children who can pick out a picture in a book after listening to the description of its main characteristics will eventually learn to discriminate between pictures that differ only slightly. Gradually, as their visual discrimination sharpens, they will be able to identify the different letters.

❑ Following Directions

Children must develop the skill of following oral directions before they can follow written directions.

❑ Developing Eye-Hand Coordination—Guiding a Pencil

Eye-hand coordination is an essential reading readiness skill that toddlers start to develop when they use thick crayons and paper. However, since most two-year-olds are independent and want to do everything by themselves, two is not the best age to show a child how to hold a crayon.

Around three, young children may well be eager to imitate how an adult holds a crayon or pencil. Then let children try the tracing and drawing activities suggested later in this chapter. Adults must be patient. It takes time for children to learn to put the crayon down at a starting point, to go along a prescribed path, and to stop at the end. Some children need a great deal of practice before they develop the proper eye-hand coordination. Their eyes see the path, but their hands cannot steer the crayon in that direction. The adult's task is to stick to the games aspect of the activity and not to set goals for how soon children should be adept at guiding a pencil.

❑ Developing a Sense of Direction—Learning Left-to-Right Progression

Developing a sense of direction is also an important reading readiness skill. The activities suggested later teach children to move in a prescribed direction. Thus, they carefully carry out directional tasks on the concrete level as preparation for the subsequent introduction of the terms *left* and *right*. It is not advisable at this time to teach children the terms *right* and *left*; there is time for teaching them these names when they are five or six, after they have developed a sense of direction.

It has been my experience that a great many children need a very long time—sometimes one to two years—to develop this sense of direction; yet it has to be learned, since reading requires the ability to move the eyes in one direction only, from left to right.

All of these readiness skills can be developed by playing games. Although it is impossible to give an exact time schedule for starting these games, children's success as learners makes it vital that they experience early, around age three, the feelings of competence and confidence that come with completing a specific task. These experiences help to lay the foundation for reading readiness. Children want to learn because they enjoy the resultant feelings of mastery.

Take children's behavior as a signal for which games to try. If they enjoy following oral directions such as "Please put these spoons on the table," they are probably ready for listening games such as Do What the Puppet Does or the Command Game. If they are constantly scribbling with a pencil or a crayon, try the games Follow the Arrow with Your Pencil or Put In What Is Missing.

Use the following games as a source of suggestions rather than as a rigid agenda. Don't play more than one or two games a day. What is most important is that you and the children enjoy playing together. Many of these games lend themselves well to group games, birthday parties, or family outings. Some of the games are adapted from Maria Montessori, who used them to develop certain readiness skills in preschool children.

GAMES THAT DEVELOP LISTENING SKILLS AND CONCENTRATION

1. LISTENING GAME. How to play: Ask youngsters to close their eyes. They must tell you what noises they hear from the street and who makes them: the honking of a car, people talking, the rustling of leaves, the chirping of birds, the barking of a dog. This game requires no preparation and is a great favorite with children.

2. WHAT MADE THE NOISE? How to play: Place several objects such as a pencil, spoon, glass, pot, piece of paper, and wooden spoon on a small table. Ask one child to close her eyes. Make a noise by tapping the pencil against the table and ask her how you made the noise. Or ring the spoon against the glass, or later, the wooden spoon against the pot. Or rustle the paper. Ask, "How did I make the noise?"

3. TAPPING A RHYTHM. How to play: Tap simple rhythms on a drum or with a wooden spoon on a pot and ask a child to repeat it. Start with no more than two or three taps so that children will be successful when they imitate you.

4. WHERE IS THE ALARM CLOCK? How to play: Take a small alarm clock that ticks noticeably and hide it. Children should find it by listening for the ticking. After a while, you can make the game more difficult by extending your realm to two rooms.

GAMES THAT EXPAND SPEAKING VOCABULARY

5. RIDDLE GAME. How to play: Say, for instance, "I am thinking of something you wear on Halloween. You wear it on your face." Or "I am thinking of something you wear in bad weather. You wear them on your feet."

6. RHYMING GAME. How to play: Make up riddles in which the answer rhymes with a word you provide, for instance, "I'm thinking of something that rhymes with *fat*. It is an animal that meows." You can easily explain what rhyming means by referring to the nursery rhymes children know. Ask if *cap* and *nap* rhyme.

GAMES THAT DEVELOP OBSERVATIONAL SKILL AND CONCENTRATION

7. I SEE SOMETHING. How to play: Start out by saying, "I see something that is red, and it is in this room." Children will guess various objects and finally hit on the right one. If necessary, help them by giving an additional clue, for example, "You can sit on it." Inevitably, the children will want their turn to give you a riddle.

8. GRAB BAG GAME. Preparation: Put three or four toys or objects in a grab bag. They must be of different shapes and sizes, for instance, a ball, a comb, a doll, and a spoon.

How to play: Ask children to close their eyes, reach into the grab bag, and get hold of one object. They are to feel the object and tell you what they have in their hands without looking at it. They can then check it to see if they are right.

The game can be made easier if children watch and see which objects you put in the bag, or it can be made harder if they have no idea of what is in the bag.

9. MATCH THE COLOR. Preparation: Put four spools of different colored threads on your tray. Place four identical spools in a nearby room or on a table far removed from your tray.

How to play: Ask children to choose one of the spools on your tray, look at it closely, and name its color (help them if necessary). Now they should put the spool down, go to the place where the matching spools are placed, and pick the same color without looking back at your tray. They then bring the spool to you to check if it is the same as the one they originally chose on your tray.

10. WHAT DID I TAKE AWAY? Hiding games are splendid for lengthening ability to concentrate and developing powers of observation and resourcefulness. Children find these games most enjoyable.

How to play: Put four objects or toys on a tray. Ask a child to name and describe them. Then ask him to close his eyes. Take one of the objects away and ask, "What did I take away?"

Variation: You can make this more difficult by using five objects. Or while a child's eyes are closed, take one toy away and put a new one in its place. Now ask, "What did I take away and what new toy did I put in its place?"

11. WHERE IS THE THIMBLE? How to play: Hide a thimble in one room; then call children and ask them to find it. If you notice that they are getting discouraged, give them helpful hints such as "You are getting warmer."

12. WHICH CUP HAS THE TOY? How to play: Put four paper cups on a tray. The cups must be exactly alike. Hide a small toy, for example, a little fish, under one of the cups while a child watches you. Now move the cups around, always moving two cups at a time. Let go of those two cups and move two different cups. The child's eyes must stay glued to the cup where the toy is hidden. Finally, stop and ask the child to point to the cup where the toy is hidden.

13. FIND THE PICTURE. How to play: Choose a picture book that has very clean, uncluttered illustrations. Have one of the children sit opposite you, so she can't see the picture you are looking at. Describe what you see: "I see two children on a horse; in the back are a rooster and some hens." Now close the book, hand it to the youngster and have her find the picture. Here, too, there is a progression from easy to difficult if you first choose a book the children know and eventually use a book they do not know. In the example cited above, the task is easy if only one page has children on a horse. It is hard if several pages show children on a horse, but only one has a rooster and hens in the background.

GAMES THAT DEVELOP SKILLS IN FOLLOWING DIRECTIONS

14. STOP WHEN THE MUSIC STOPS. How to play: On the piano play a simple tune, or tap a rhythm on a drum or other object. At times play very softly so the children have to listen attentively. The children walk to the music, but the instant you stop, they have to stop in whatever position they find themselves. They cannot take even half a step.

Variation: Four- or five-year-olds may want to learn to skip to the music. Teach them to skip slowly, showing them in slow steps how to lift their feet alternately. Then they can skip to the music. Again, they have to stop when the music stops. This time they are allowed to bring their feet down to the floor.

15. DO WHAT THE PUPPET DOES. How to play: Hold a puppet or doll in your hands; it should face you as the children do. When you make the puppet jump up and down, the children must imitate it exactly. When your puppet lifts its left arm or right foot, so must the children, and so on.

While young children enjoy the challenge of obeying these directions, these games are also helpful in developing a sense of direction.

16. COMMAND GAME. This marvelous readiness game not only develops the ability to listen well, but also trains children to remember a sequence of verbal commands.

How to play: You begin by asking children to play the command game. Say to one child, "Go to my desk, get the stack of papers, and give one paper to each of the children. Then go back to your chair and sit down." At home, parents can say, "Listen carefully. I want you to bring me a spoon from the kitchen, then I want you to close the door to the bedroom, and then I want you to sit down on the floor, right in front of me." The children must follow your "commands" in the exact order in which you have given them.

Variation: Obviously, you can make the game simpler by giving only two commands at first or harder by eventually giving four commands. Five or six commands make the task challenging for any five-year-old.

GAMES THAT DEVELOP EYE-HAND COORDINATION AND A SENSE OF DIRECTION

17. FOLLOW THE ARROW. How to play: With chalk, draw a large circle on the classroom or kitchen floor. Tell children they must walk exactly on the chalk line. Next draw an arrow alongside the circle: the children must walk in the direction of the arrow. Erase the arrow, and draw another arrow pointing in the opposite direction. Let a child trace over your line with chalk. This is a good game to play in the yard or on the sidewalk or on the beach.

Variation: You can combine this game with Stop When the Music Stops by having children stop walking the instant you stop tapping the drum.

18. FOLLOW THE ARROW WITH YOUR PENCIL. Preparation: Draw a faint line across a sheet of paper. Now place an arrow above the line at the left.

How to play: Children should trace your line with their pencils in the prescribed direction, from left to right.
This activity develops eye-hand coordination and a sense of direction, as well as dexterity in using a pencil.

Variation: You can make this activity more interesting by cutting out pictures or drawing pictures that have a sensible connection (see figure 7.1). This variation also provides an opportunity for enriching

Figure 7.1 Follow the arrow with your pencil.

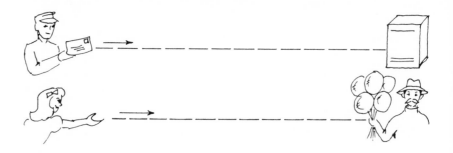

Figure 7.2 Finish the drawing.

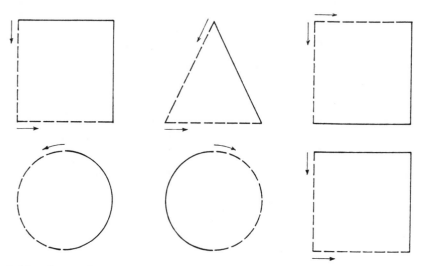

children's speaking vocabularies, for they can make up a story about each set of drawings.

19. FINISH THE DRAWING. Preparation: Draw a series of incomplete circles, squares, and triangles (see figure 7.2). Place an arrow next to the dotted line indicating to children that they should trace the line in the prescribed direction. Completing a circle is good preparation for writing letters that have curves.

How to play: Going from row to row, let the children identify the two geometric figures that are alike. This develops their observation, simultaneously providing them with practice for developing eye-hand coordination and a sense of direction. If they want to, they can even learn the names of the geometric figures. They can also color the two figures that are alike.

20. PUT IN WHAT IS MISSING. Preparation: Make very simple drawings, leaving out an important item. Suggestions: a face without a mouth, a doll with one leg, a bicycle with one tire, and so on (see figure 7.3).

How to play: The children figure out what is missing and draw it in.

In conclusion, it is important to stress that the time in children's lives *when* you consciously start nurturing general reading readiness is inextricably tied in with *how* you start and with the emotional and intellectual atmosphere around the children. The home environment as well as the preschool classroom should be the "good earth" from which all learning flows.

Learning to listen attentively, for instance, is possible for children who have been given relatively few commands, and these in a firm, friendly voice which they respect and have learned to hear. Children who are shouted at constantly learn to tune out the grown-up.

It is necessary to have clearly defined rules in daily living to give children the security of knowing what to expect and who they are. Children have to accept brushing their teeth as inevitable, even on days when they do not feel like it or when they are too tired. But learning and intellectual curiosity are different from the routines and habits your children have to acquire. The desire to learn springs creatively from children's natural curiosity; it cannot be forced. Avoid a head-on collision over any activity related to books and learning. If you refrain from disciplining children in these matters, they'll keep the feeling that learning is exciting and rewarding in itself.

Figure 7.3 Put in what is missing.

8
Readiness Games for Four-year-olds

Before proceeding with the games described in this chapter, assess how well children have mastered the games presented in chapter 7. For an informal evaluation of their progress, use the games described in chapter 7. If the children can do them easily, they have the foundation to develop the skills that we will be dealing with here. If they cannot do them, continue playing the games from chapter 7 for another month or two until the children have mastered them.

❑ Understanding Sequence

Understanding that events happen sequentially is an important reading readiness skill, because in spoken words, sounds occur sequentially: in the word *man* you hear the sounds /m/ and /ă/ /n/ in that order. Correspondingly, in written words, the letters have a sequential order.

❑ Classifying

Seeing different objects as belonging to a common category is a challenge to children's intelligence. As a matter of fact, classifying was tested in the early intelligence tests. It can and should be developed in four- and five-year-olds. Most four-year-olds enjoy this new way of looking at objects. A spoon, knife, and fork, although they have different names and are different visually, all belong to the category of eating utensils. Later, children will apply this ability to spoken words: *mitten, milk,* and *mirror,* although they have completely different meanings, all begin with /m/.

❑ Developing Fine Auditory Discrimination— Specifically, Identifying Initial Sounds of Spoken Words

This skill must be mastered before going on to the next two skills. Children must be able to *hear* the initial sound of *man* before they see the corresponding letter *m*.

The games that follow will help develop the readiness skills described. All of these games present a definite task to be mastered. Thus, they present a challenge to children and are not boring to children and adults alike.

Developing these readiness skills should be done only in a relaxed play milieu that is enjoyable to you and the children. The following list of suggested games and activities is not intended as a rigid agenda. Look at it as a resource file to draw on. It is more important that everyone enjoys playing the games than that you be concerned about how many games are played each day. Choose one of the appropriate games and then, if the children want more, you can try a second one.

GAMES THAT REVIEW EYE-HAND COORDINATION AND A SENSE OF DIRECTION

Children must be able to hold a pencil and draw lines before going on to writing letters. Hopefully your children have developed some fine motor control with the tracing games described in chapter 7.

It is equally essential that children have learned to move in a prescribed direction before they start learning letters.

A sense of direction is crucial, not only in learning to read and write, but in identifying and writing a letter. If children have a tendency to go in the opposite direction, play one tracing game each day, so that gradually, they develop a sense of direction. Use the appropriate games outlined in this chapter. As mentioned in chapter 5, nothing in a preschooler's life helps them to develop this sense of direction, yet it must be developed *before* children learn sound-letter correspondence.

1. FOLLOW THE ARROW. How to play: Make the tracing activities more challenging by requiring longer lines. Be sure children know that they have to be drawn in a prescribed direction (see figure 8.1).

2. FOLLOW THE DOTS. How to play: Let children draw lines, starting at the arrow, to connect the dots. Use arrows to indicate left-to-right direction and remind them to go in the direction of the arrows (see figure 8.2).

Figure 8.1 Follow the arrow with your pencil.

GAMES THAT DEVELOP THE ABILITY TO CLASSIFY

3. WHICH OF THESE TOYS BELONG TOGETHER? Preparation: Form a collection of inexpensive toys and objects, for example, a lion, tiger, mouse, and fork.

How to play: Ask a child, "Which of these toys belong together?" Help them to realize that the toys are all animals, but that the fork, an eating utensil, is different. Now put a knife, fork, spoon, and a book on the tray. Which things go together? Which does not belong in the group? What are the objects called? Turning it into a game, put a miscellaneous collection of objects on a table nearby. Now put three animals on your tray and ask a child to find something on the table that will fit into the category (toy mouse or toy lion, for instance).

4. WHAT DOES NOT BELONG? How to play: Put five toys on a tray with one article of clothing, perhaps a mitten. Ask a child to look at the things on your tray and to take off the object that does not belong. If a child responds correctly by taking off the mitten, ask him to tell you which category (toys, or things to play with) the objects on your tray belong to.

Variation: Or you can play the same game by using pictures cut from magazines and pasted on large index cards. You can make the game more intriguing by using more subtle categories—for example, you can have pictures of four children playing and one sleeping. Ask, "Which picture does not belong?" Children will remove the picture of the sleeping child and state the category: children who play.

As you collect more pictures, reverse roles and let a child choose the category and put you to the test.

Figure 8.2 Follow the dots with your pencil.

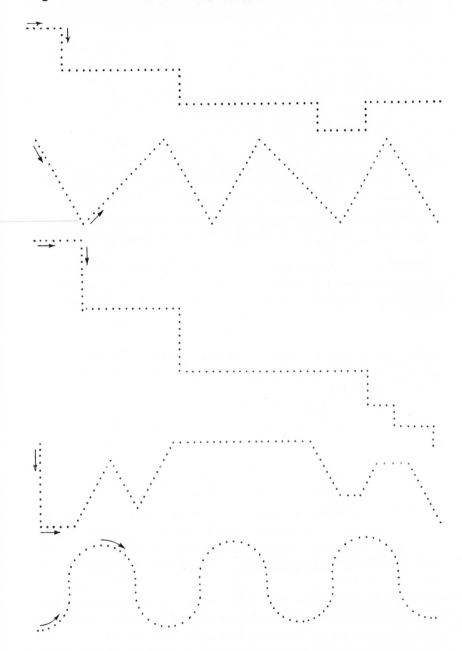

GAMES THAT DEVELOP AN UNDERSTANDING OF SEQUENCE

Understanding sequence is an important readiness skill. In order to read, children must be able to sound out a word according to the sequence of the letters, and in order to write they must record in sequence the sounds they hear. Later they must be able to grasp the sequence of a story to be good readers.

5. WHICH COMES FIRST? Preparation: To play a sequence game, draw or cut out pictures that tell a story—for example, show the picture of a cake mix and the picture of a finished cake.

How to play: Put both pictures in front of a child and ask her to place the pictures in order from left to right. Which comes first?

Variation: You can make the task more difficult by using three or four pictures that have a logical sequence. First, place the pictures in their proper sequence and have a child tell the story they portray. Then scramble the pictures and have the child arrange them in their logical sequence. Suggestions: 1) Snow falling, a child dragging a sled out of doors, pulling it uphill, sledding downhill. 2) A child in bed, getting dressed, having breakfast, taking a school bus, sitting in a kindergarten room.

Animals provide natural sequence stories and, incidentally, offer information about nature. You might use the following:

egg	chick	hen
moth	spinning cocoon	butterfly
bee	beehive	honey
beaver	collecting twigs	building a dam

The most important step in the systematic development of reading readiness will be helping children discover the correspondence of sounds and letters. This teaching falls naturally into two parts: first, identifying initial sounds of familiar words; second, recording these sounds by letters. I have found that it is important to teach auditory discrimination first. Many sound games should be played before children learn how these sounds are recorded by letters. Hence, in this chapter only games that develop auditory discrimination are described. No written letters will be introduced as yet. Only after children have mastered the skill of auditory discrimination will they learn (in chapter 9) how these sounds are recorded by letters.

GAMES THAT DEVELOP AUDITORY DISCRIMINATION

Not overlooking the possibility that some children are ready to play these games at age three and a half, I recommend that teachers and parents start these games no later than age four. Since the games involve concrete objects and toys, most four-year-olds enjoy playing them. Some children need a great deal of time to develop auditory discrimination.

Below are listed a number of games to help children develop auditory discrimination, specifically the skill of identifying the initial sound of words familiar to them. Occasionally, children may give the alphabet name of the letter even in these sound games. Remind them to listen to the initial sound. They themselves will realize that they do not hear the alphabet name at the beginning of spoken words.

6. WHAT DO I WANT? How to play: Put a number of objects on a tray. The names of all the objects should start with different sounds—mitten, candle, feather, and apple. Name each object, emphasizing the initial sound. (In *apple* you hear the short sound /ă/, not the long sound /ā/.) Now tell the children you are going to ask them to pick up the object you want from the tray. You won't say its full name but will call for the object by the sound that starts its name. For instance, you might say, "The name of the thing I want begins with /f/." The children must pick up the feather.

7. RIDDLE GAME WITH PICTURES. How to play: For this game, choose a book with pictures of clearly illustrated objects. Hand the book to a child and ask him to find the animal you can ride on. Its name starts with /h/. Or ask a child to show you an animal that barks. Its name starts with /d/.

8. I SEE SOMETHING. How to play: This is a new version of an old favorite. For instance, say, "I see something. You sit on it. Its name starts with /ch/." Some time later encourage children to think up a riddle on their own.

9. I THINK OF SOMETHING. How to play: This is a harder version of the Riddle Game described in chapter 7—a good game to play in the car. Say, for instance, "I am thinking of something that you can see only in the sky, and its name begins with /m/." Children must think through that moon, sun, or stars would fit the first part of the riddle, but only moon fits both specifications.

10. COMMAND GAME WITH INITIAL SOUNDS. How to play: "Ask your neighbor for something that starts with /p/ (pencil). . . . Then go to the desk and get me the /b/ (book) that is lying there. . . . Then go to the cupboard and get something that starts with /c/ (cup)."

11. WHAT DID I TAKE AWAY? Preparation: Collect several toys and objects. At first, use only things whose names start with the sounds /m/, /f/, and /l/. For instance, put a mirror, magnet, fork, and lion on a tray.

How to play: Ask a child to lift up each object, one at a time, say its name, and see if she can tell you the very first sound the name starts with. Repeat after her the name *mirror*, for example, emphasizing strongly its initial sound so she can hear the sound better. Now ask her to close her eyes while you take one object away. Let us suppose you take the magnet away. When she opens her eyes, ask her to tell you what you removed. She will miss the magnet. Then encourage her to explain what the magnet is used for and to say its first sound.

This is an all-time favorite among children. After a while, they especially enjoy taking turns as the "teacher."

12. PARTNERS GAME. How to play: Put three objects on a tray, two of them starting with the same sound, one of them not. Have children pick out the partners. For instance, lion and lollipop start with /l/, fork does not. An older child will want to reverse roles.

13. WHICH TOY DOES NOT BELONG? How to play: Put on a tray three or four toys, objects, or pictures of objects that all start with the same sound, and one extra that does not. For instance, put a mirror, marble, magnet, and feather on the tray. A child will pick out the feather as not belonging.

Once you use this classifying game for identifying sounds, you may not use it any more for other classifying games because children may become confused. Its new purpose is to teach initial sounds.

14. FIND PICTURES. This game and the next one are harder and thus perhaps more suitable for five-year-olds.

How to play: Give a child a magazine or a mail-order catalog, and ask him to find (and later cut out) pictures that start with /m/. Later ask for pictures whose names start with /f/, and still later with /l/.

15. TELL A STORY. How to play: Tell a simple story, leaving out the nouns, except for their initial sounds. For instance, "Denise woke up in the m——. The s—— was shining. She brushed her t——." As you go along, the children supply the missing noun. Give them additional hints if they need them. When children are able to hear and identify the initial sounds of almost any word, then they are ready to learn the sound names of the letters.

Suppose your children can play these games effortlessly, that is, they are really able to hear and identify the initial sound of any word. At this point you have to decide whether they are ready for the next step, the recording of these sounds by letters. How will you know if a child has reached the critical period for dealing with symbolic abstractions? The next chapter will tell you.

SUGGESTIONS FOR CHILDREN WITH DIFFICULTIES

☐ SPECIAL HELP FOR DEVELOPING EYE-HAND COORDINATION

Some four-year-old children find it extremely difficult to do tracing activities. Some have to begin by learning how to hold a crayon. Let them study the position of your fingers when you hold one and have them copy you.

Some children have trouble guiding the crayon with their eyes. Being able to start at a designated point and end at another is hard for them and takes time and practice. You can simplify the tracing activity by omitting the arrow, having instead a very heavy starting line and a heavy dot to mark the finish. You can make a raised beginning and end with clay if you think that *feeling* the beginning and end would help.

❑ Special Help for Developing a Sense of Direction

There are children who require a long time to develop a sense of direction. They consistently draw lines from right to left even though the starting line is marked. They need to overlearn in this area. If you have children who have difficulties with tracing in a prescribed direction, draw a chalk line on the class or kitchen floor. Use a basket or a chair as the agreed-upon starting point. At the end of the line put a little toy. At your signal the children have to walk on the line, starting at the basket or chair and proceeding to the toy. They may then pick up the toy and keep it. They will want to play again!

Next, give children practice in tracing dotted lines from left to right. Mark the starting point with a heavy red line. Draw or cut pictures that will create a meaningful relationship between start and finish. Examples are shown in figure 8.3.

Do not teach children the terms *left* and *right*. This will only confuse them. Your aim is to get children used to the idea that they are to move in only *one* prescribed direction. For this goal they do not need to know that they are, in fact, always moving from left to right.

❑ Special Help for Developing Auditory Discrimination

Some children need special help to develop auditory discrimination. If children have difficulty hearing and understanding that *mitten* begins with /m/, follow these steps:

Figure 8.3 Follow the dotted line.

Step 1: Tell children that *mitten* begins with the sound /m/ and that *man* begins with /m/. Use as many examples of words beginning with /m/ as are necessary for them to hear the /m/ sound.

Step 2: Seat children opposite you to play a new game with you. Put on a tray only toys whose names start with /m/. One child chooses a toy and says its name. Tell him your hand will go up to signal *stop*. When your hand goes up, the child must stop saying the word. Raise your hand the instant the child says the /m/ sound in *mitten* or *man*. If you use only words that start with /m/, the child will catch on.

Step 3: Now use the other games that develop auditory discrimination as described in this chapter, but use only toys whose names start with /m/. Once children can identify the initial sound for these toys, use the same steps in helping children hear the initial sound /f/. Now use only toys whose names start with /f/.

Step 4: Next, combine toys whose names start with either /m/ or /f/. If children can identify the initial sounds of their names, you have helped them enormously.

Proceed slowly, introducing each new sound by using toys—later pictures—with only the new sound. Simplify the task by using only the new sound and the preceding sound that children have learned. At the end of chapter 9 you'll find the sequence in which to teach letters; use the same sequence in teaching sounds now.

If you find that in spite of this extra practice, children have difficulties in any one of these areas, stop working with them temporarily. At this point I suggest that children have a thorough checkup.

- I recommend that a child's hearing, vision, and speech be checked; parents can ask their pediatrician where to take the child. Children have usually outgrown their baby speech by the age of four, so it is wise to have their enunciation checked at this stage as well.

- You may wish to get an outside psychological evaluation by a psychologist who believes in early intervention rather than by one who says, "Don't worry; they'll outgrow these problems in time."

Don't keep on teaching readiness skills if there is no progress. Children will sense your apprehension and this is more detrimental than a postponement of learning. It may be that a psychologist will suggest outside tutoring rather than parental teaching to help children overcome their difficulties. Outside help is more advantageously used now than later, after a child experiences difficulties in school. The vast majority of four-year-olds who have learning disabilities in a specific area can learn a particular skill if they are given enough time and practice, provided the help is given before they develop feelings of discouragement and failure.

SPECIAL SUGGESTIONS FOR CLASSES MADE UP OF DISADVANTAGED CHILDREN WITH LEARNING DISABILITIES

There are situations where all of the readiness skills have to be developed quite late when the children are already in first grade. After my first year as reading consultant in the Newark Eighteenth Avenue School, the principal asked me if, in the coming year, I would take on the lowest exponent of the first grade (I had an HEW grant and was only responsible for my experimental class). I agreed. Most of those children had not had any kindergarten experiences. Also, most of them had been diagnosed as learning disabled.

When I started helping the teacher in the fall, it became clear that we had to start at the very beginning. We had to teach the children how to speak in full sentences and how to hold a pencil. We had to develop their auditory discrimination and their sense of direction: in short, we had to develop every one of the necessary readiness skills.

I asked for a puppet theater and was given a deluxe one. Only those children who could speak in full sentences could participate in a puppet show (we modeled full sentences for them to show the difference from mere phrases). The children's English improved markedly as the puppet shows became favorites. Also, the children learned to follow directions, especially when given by the "stage director."

We made sure that the teacher had one small group of about six children at a time to teach readiness skills to. We installed several interest centers containing easels, clay, records, and water toys. By the end of the year, all of the children could read short-a words, an accomplishment never before achieved in the school! Mothers came into the classroom with tears in their eyes, because now, for the first time, one of their children could read. By the end of third grade, when I visited them, all of the children read fluently. The experiment had worked!

9
Discovering Letters and Sounds

•••

Helping children discover the sound-letter relationships is an exciting adventure. In all probability, your children have been curious about written language for quite some time. They may have evidenced this by scribbling on paper and then telling you what they have written. But now you will help them progress from this make-believe activity to the reality of learning that the letter *m*, for example, represents the sound they hear at the beginning of *monkey* and *mitten*. The squiggle on paper—a specific letter—now says something!

For children to be able to learn this sound-letter relationship, two things are required: neurological maturation and the development of all the previous reading readiness skills we have been discussing.

Neurological maturation is necessary for the brain to make the connection between the auditory input of the initial sound and the visual input of the corresponding written letter. A common analogy compares the brain to a central switchboard in the telephone system; the brain connects auditory and visual stimuli, registering the connection. Children are able to realize that the /m/ sound they hear at the beginning of *man* is recorded by the letter *m*, or that the letter *m* represents the sound /m/ heard at the beginning of words like *mirror* and *mask*.

Recalling the list of readiness skills at the start of chapter 7, we see that children now have two more skills to master.

❑ Understanding Sound-Letter Correspondence

Understanding sound-letter correspondence is a complicated learning process. Some children need a very long time, up to seven or eight months, to begin to understand this correspondence.

❑ Developing Fine Visual Discrimination— Specifically, Identifying Letters

To many children, letters like *l* and *f* look very much alike; it may take them a long time to be able to pick out the critical features of *all* the letters.

WHEN TO INTRODUCE SOUNDS AND LETTERS

Even if children are exceptionally bright, disregard those books that recommend teaching reading to two-year-olds. Don't teach even three-year-olds the letters of the alphabet. They are not neurologically mature enough to understand their meaning, nor have they mastered the readiness skills necessary for learning to read. The age of three is the optimum age for playing the readiness games outlined in chapter 7.

In a good learning environment, most four-and-a-half-year-olds and even four-year-olds, for that matter, have mastered all the necessary readiness skills and have matured to the point that they can understand sound-letter correspondence. At this age they also show an avid interest in written language. Start children who are approximately four years old with one of the following games that teach sound-letter correspondence at a leisurely pace. Observe the children. If they do not want to stop as soon as you start, but ask to play more of these games, they are ready for this new phase of learning. If the game seems too hard and the children do not understand, stop. You can always try again a few months later.

In kindergarten at the latest, children should start on games that let them discover sounds and letters. Natural readers should not wait beyond five, for they easily pass the critical period. Neither should children with poor visual discrimination or perceptual problems start after five. They need at least one full year to learn some of the letters, and they should learn them before they enter first grade, as slowly as they need to.

At this point you may want to give children my readiness book for four- and five-year-olds entitled *The Great Adventure: Getting Ready to Read.* This is the first in a set of ten readiness books that develops all the readiness skills discussed here. It also teaches the first four letters in the Structural Reading sequence, intelligibly, successfully, and amusingly.

Some children, like Bobby and Robin, need an extraordinarily long time, eight to ten months, to learn the critical features of one letter and distinguish them from those of another. These children do not magically develop this ability when they enter first grade. It must be developed early, at a time when there is neither pressure nor anxiety about learning.

Don't be concerned about how fast children learn in this area.

The number of letters children learn before they go to first grade is unimportant. What matters is their understanding of the relationship between sounds and letters. If they know only six initial sounds and their corresponding letters, they have already mastered a crucial readiness skill.

❑ Sequence of Letters

At the end of this chapter is a model of the size of each letter children will write. Figures 9.4 and 9.5 show how to start writing each letter by accentuating the starting point and the sequence in which to teach the letters. Because the traditional alphabetical sequence is not used, children will not fall into the habit of blindly reciting the ABCs. The sequence of letters was chosen on the basis of ease in auditory discrimination. The /m/, /f/, /l/, and /ă/ are the first four letters taught because children can easily distinguish their sounds. In contrast, /m/ and /n/, which are adjacent in the alphabet, sound similar and are harder to distinguish; therefore, they should be separated by several other letters.

❑ Letter Picture Cards

Each letter is first introduced with its letter picture card. This is the single most important teaching device throughout the process of learning letters. The device of a letter picture makes learning each letter meaningful to children. Each letter is embedded in its picture. As children say the name of that picture, they identify its initial sound and then can deduce what the letter on top of the picture says. Using the spoken word as a starting point creates a meaningful relationship between sound and letter.

The letter picture card is a self-teaching device. If children are unsure about a letter, all they have to do is find its letter picture card and say its name. By identifying its initial sound, they find the sound name of the letter.

❑ Toys and Pictures

For practicing sound-letter correspondence you will use toys, pictures, and picture card games. As children progress you may want to rely more on pictures than on toys. Early on, children may become fascinated with the card games, described in the following section, in preference to all other games.

While playing any of the sound-letter or later reading games, make sure that you always sit alongside children, never across from them, unless otherwise specified.

GAMES THAT DEVELOP SOUND-LETTER KNOWLEDGE

At this point, parents and teachers may find it expedient to start the Structural Reading Book, *We Discover Sounds and Letters* (see "Learning Materials for Reading Readiness and Reading" in Appendix). This book will help children develop all of the readiness skills. It will also teach children ten letters through tracing only. No freehand writing is required. The following is a list of games to help children understand sound-letter correspondence; they can be adapted to any letter or letters. We will start out with these four: *m, f, l,* and *a*. When children have mastered them, prepare the children for the next four (see end of chapter for letter sequence). To play these games, you need to do the following three things:

- To make your own letter picture cards, choose a picture whose name starts with the sound you want to teach. Let's say you have drawn or cut out a picture of a mitten; paste it on a 5″ × 8″ index card. Then write with a blue magic marker a lowercase *m* on top of the picture, 1¼″ tall. The picture should be in outline form, preferably in black, so the letter stands out in the foreground (for samples see figure 9.1).

  As you prepare letter picture cards for subsequent letters, keep in mind that there is a difference in height between letters. Please use only the following sizes:

  1¼″: m a s c n i r o e u v w x z
  1¾″: p g j q y
  2″ : f l t h b k d

- Collect objects or toys whose names start with the sounds you are going to teach the children. At the end of this chapter you will also find suggestions for which toys or objects to use.
- To prepare for card games, make a set of picture cards. Cut a number of 3″ × 5″ index cards in half. Look for similar sized, realistic pictures in catalogs and magazines (mail order catalogs provide a wealth of pictures), and paste one picture on each half of the index

Figure 9.1 Letter pictures for *m, f, l,* and *a*

card. You need five different pictures for every sound you are going to teach.

In addition, you need to write five plain letters on the same size card (one half of a 3″ × 5″ index card) to correspond to the five pictures you have selected for each letter. For instance, write five *m*s for the five *m*-pictures, such as mouse, mail carrier, mirror, magnet, and marble. Use the same size as you did for the letter picture cards. Always write the vowels in red and the consonants in blue.

❏ Expanding Children's Vocabularies

Some of the objects or pictures suggested at the end of the chapter may well be unfamiliar to children. I have purposely included such objects as *ferry* or *ambulance* to enrich children's speaking vocabularies and broaden their knowledge. Identify each object and talk about its use. Through such discussions their terminology will grow more precise; for instance, if they can't distinguish between a mitten and a glove, you can help them understand the difference.

❑ Introducing the Letter *m*

Put the letter picture card for *m* before a child, who should identify the picture as a mitten. Now, slowly tracing the blue lines of the letter with your finger, explain that these lines form the letter that says /m/, the first sound in *mitten*. Let the children trace the letter with their fingers. Be sure they start at the top of the letter and proceed to trace it in the correct direction, from left to right.

1. PICK OUT THE CORRECT TOYS. How to play: Place the letter picture card for *m* upright in front of the children. Prop it up between two blocks or small boxes. Set up on a nearby chair or table your collection of toys whose names begin with the sounds /m/, /l/, and /f/. Ask a child to pick out only those toys that start with /m/ and to place them in front of the letter picture card for *m*. It is entirely possible that some children have learned the alphabet names of the letters somewhere. When they now see the letter *m*, they'll call it /em/. You don't have to say, "This is wrong." Just remind them to listen to the sound they hear. Children relearn rather quickly to give the sound name of the letter, and their knowledge of the alphabet name will fade into the background.

If children are able to play this game of picking out the correct toys, you can now go on to the Letter-Tracing Game.

2. LETTER-TRACING GAME WITH ONE LETTER. Preparation: Prepare sheets of paper on which you write the *m*s in dots. Draw a heavy line to indicate where children should start each letter.

How to play: Now explain, "If I say a word that starts with /m/ like *mitten*, you may trace one *m*. If I say another word, like *daddy* or *school*, you must not move your pencils. Since these words do not start with /m/, you cannot trace an *m*."

In all tracing and writing games I use lined, commercial notebook paper (the largest width). In order to help children learn to align their letters properly, I first prepare the page using three spaces defined by four lines. The two middle lines (which are to contain the body, or core, of each letter) are drawn with dark lines. The top line for the "up" letters and the bottom line for the "down" letters are drawn in lighter lines. Each horizontal "staff" of four lines is then separated by two spaces, so that it stands out clearly (see figure 9.2).

For proper development of the readiness skills, it is important that children do not trace the *m*s unless you are supervising them.

Figure 9.2 Letter-tracing game with one letter

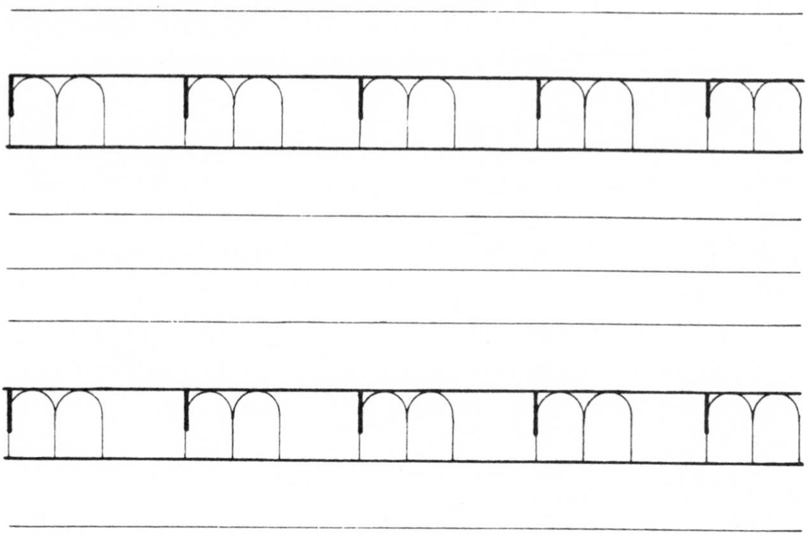

Children who have very little spatial orientation or a marked tendency toward reversals will not consistently trace the *ms* correctly. Long, hard experience has proven that from the very first tracing of a letter, children must learn to trace or write it correctly, starting at the top and proceeding in the prescribed direction. In spite of the heavy starting line indicating which way the letters go, children who lack a sense of direction frequently trace the letters incorrectly or backwards. *More harm is done if a child practices tracing the wrong way than if the child never practices it at all.* This game is most effective in helping children identify each new letter. All my preschool pupils enjoy it.

3. THE FOLDER GAME WITH INITIAL SOUNDS. Preparation: Paste two pockets side by side on a manila folder. Write *m* on one pocket and *f* on the other. Place a stack of picture cards with pictures of objects that begin with /m/ or /f/ face down in front of the children.

How to play: As children turn up a picture, they have to put it in the correct pocket.

Variation: As children learn more letters, use a folder with five handmade pockets. Write one letter to be mastered on each pocket.

4. THE MAIL CARRIER. Preparation: Place the $m, f, l,$ and a letter picture cards between blocks so they are upright in front of the children. Have your collection of toys nearby. The child chosen to be the mail carrier can be given a mail carrier's hat and bag to make the game more playful.

How to play: Let the mail carrier select one object or toy and deliver it to the right address: the *fork* goes to the f, the *mouse* goes to the m. Any toys that begin with a different letter cannot be delivered at this time and are thus put on an empty chair, the "address unknown" place.

Variation: As a variation, you can use pictures starting with these sounds and have a child deliver each picture to the proper address. Again include foils, that is, pictures whose names start with sounds other than /m/, /f/, /l/, or /ă/.

A harder variation is to play with plain printed letters instead of letter picture cards. Have the mail carrier deliver the mail to the plain letters. However, place the corresponding letter picture cards behind the child, so if she is uncertain about a given letter, she can turn around and check by finding its letter picture card.

5. LOTTO GAME WITH PICTURES. Preparation: For this game use $5'' \times 8''$ white, unlined cards as master cards. Rule each card so you have six squares. Draw the letter with its picture in the left space of the top row. Make one master card for each of the letters to be practiced, say $m, f, l,$ and a.

How to play: From your collection, select five small picture cards whose names start with /m/, five whose names start with /f/, and so on. Give two master cards to one child and two to another child. Shuffle the small cards and place them in a pile in front of one child, who will be the caller. As he turns up a card, he will identify the picture, say its initial sound, and then both players will check to see who can claim the card. For instance, the picture of a mirror would be claimed by the player who has the m master card. The player who first fills both master cards wins.

Variation: Most children also enjoy playing the lotto game as solitaire, sorting out all the small picture cards to the proper master cards.

Later you can make this game more difficult by making new master cards, writing the letter without its letter picture in one of the squares of each card. The same small picture cards can be used with either variation of the Lotto Game.

6. SORTING GAME WITH ENVELOPES. Preparation: For this game for a child to play alone, take an ordinary manila folder and use masking tape to make a pocket inside it. On the pocket, tape one of the big *m*s you've made. Take small envelopes and put a picture in each envelope. Use some pictures of things that start with /m/ and some that do not.

How to play: Give the envelopes to the child, and ask her to open one envelope at a time. If the picture inside the envelope starts with /m/, she can place the envelope in the pocket; if not, she should discard it on a pile to the left.

When a child knows the letter *m* reasonably well and is eager to go ahead, introduce your letter picture for /f/, following the same procedure you did for /m/. Ask the child to identify the picture of the fish and to give you its initial sound (/f/). Always make sure that the child knows the meaning of each word studied. Trace the blue lines of the *f* with your finger, explaining that since this is a *f*ish, whose name starts with /f/, the blue lines form the letter *f*.

From here on, go very slowly, depending on the individual child. Some children, like Bobby and Robin, who were discussed earlier, find it very difficult to identify *m* and *f* without their letter pictures. If you feel that a child is not ready for more letters, you can play many of the following games with this child.

Always place the letter pictures, in this case *m* and *f*, first in front of, later in back of, the children so they can easily check for themselves what the letters say whenever they need to.

The letter pictures are a self-corrective tool, very much like a dictionary. If children have forgotten the sound of a given letter, they look it up in the set of letter pictures. Once they have located the letter picture, they say out loud the name of the letter picture and listen to its first sound. They hear themselves say the sound and thus, without your help, are able to deduce the sound name of the letter. They develop a sense of security knowing that they can look up a letter in case of uncertainty or to correct an error. They do not feel the burden of having to memorize a letter, nor are they subjected to the diminishing experience of being told that they are wrong or "You made a mistake."

7. MAKING A SOUND BOOK. Preparation: Manila paper or cheap drawing paper is required for this activity. Draw two lines at the bottom of the paper, and dot two rows of *m*s as you did in the Letter-Tracing Game. Be sure to make a heavy line indicating the starting point of each letter.

How to play: Ask children to tell you the sound name of the letter; then watch them trace the first letters. If they do not hesitate, let them finish the job on their own. Provide them with some old magazines and mail-order catalogs and some blunt, kindergarten scissors. Suggest that they make a sound book. Let them find pictures that start with /m/, cut them out, and paste them on the *m*-page.

On a later day you can provide the children with a page for *f*. Add pages to the sound book as the children learn new letters. After about five or six pages (many children want to do two or more pages for one letter), use a piece of colorful construction paper for a simple cover and staple it to the pages they have completed. The children have made their first book!

8. FILING PICTURES UNDER CORRECT LETTERS. Preparation: Children enjoy having a filing box. You can buy an inexpensive one that will hold 3″ × 5″ index cards, or with the children's help you can make a filing box out of an old shoe box. Put tabs on top of some index cards, which will then serve as dividers. On each tab write one of the letters the children know.

How to play: Give children an old magazine or mail catalog. They must now look for pictures whose names have initial sounds corresponding to those letters. They cut out each picture, paste it on an index card, then file it behind the proper letter.

9. GRAB BAG GAME. How to play: Have children take turns closing their eyes and picking one toy from a bag of toys. After they say the name of the toy, they put it in front of the correct letter picture card. After a while, replace these letter picture cards by index cards bearing only the letters.

Variation: Prepare sheets of paper with dotted *m*s and *f*s. A child picks out a toy and traces one *m* if its name starts with /m/, or traces one *f* if its name starts with /f/. If the name of the toy begins with any other letter, the child should identify its initial sound even though there is no corresponding letter to trace. To make the game more interesting, the children can each guess beforehand which line will win, the *m*s or the *f*s.

10. FISHING GAME. Preparation: Use metal toys with names that start with the initial sounds the children have learned. Then supply the children with a "rod" with a magnet attached to the line. Write the initial letter for each toy on plain, unlined index cards and stand the cards on the table. Put the toys in a box.

How to play: Give the children turns "fishing" without looking into the box. When they have caught a toy, they must tell you its initial sound, then place the toy in front of the correct letter.

This game requires some preparation and thought, but is very well liked by many children and can be used again and again.

11. BALL PITCHING GAME. Preparation: Label three or four cardboard boxes with the latest letters the children have learned, using plain white paper labels and the letters without their letter pictures. Set the boxes in a row, and let the children take turns standing at a designated place, about eight to ten feet away. Provide a ball or a beanbag.

How to play: When you say a word, for instance, *apple*, a child has to identify the initial sound orally, then throw the ball into the correct box, in this case, the *a*-box.

12. HOPSCOTCH. Preparation: Draw a hopscotch diagram on the playground or sidewalk. Label each square with a letter the children have learned.

How to play: One child hops to the first square and puts his feet down. If he can think of a word that starts with that sound, he can hop to the next square. Again, he has to think of something that starts with the sound of that letter before he can hop to the next square. The child who first reaches the last hopscotch square wins.

Variation: The children can try to hop from square to square, saying out loud the appropriate words without stopping to put both feet down.

13. LETTER-TRACING GAME WITH TWO OR MORE LET-TERS. Games involving the tracing of letters are the single most effective activity in reinforcing children's visual discrimination. The kinesthetic experience of tracing makes children aware of the differences between letters: they *feel* the letters, and this feeling subsequently enables them to *identify* the letters.

Many children experience difficulty in merely *seeing* the differences between letters that to them appear very similar.

Preparation: Prepare a red and blue lined sheet as you did in the previous Letter-Tracing Game. Now dot two lines of *m*s and two lines of *f*s. Indicate with heavy crayon where the letter should start.

How to play: Explain to the children that if you say a word that starts with /f/—for instance, *fork*—they may trace one *f.* If you say a word that starts with /m/, they may trace one *m.* If you say a word that starts with any other sound, they should not move their pencils. As each child learns more letters, you can adapt this Letter-Tracing Game, always using the last four letters studied.

Whenever a child needs practice in tracing a particular letter, use this game or variations of it rather than having a child trace row after row of letters.

This game is a favorite of children who concentrate on playing. They don't realize how often they have traced a given letter.

14. MATCHING GAME. Preparation: Cut unlined 3″ × 5″ index cards in half. Write one *m* on each of five cards, and write one *f* on each of five cards. Help the children find and cut out five pictures that start with /m/ and five pictures that start with /f/. Paste each picture on half an index card.

How to play: Now combine the letter cards and picture cards, shuffle them, and place them face down between the players. Have them take turns picking up one card. The picture cards should go to the right side of the table, the letter cards to the left. If one child turns up the picture card of a fork and there is a letter card with *f* on the table, she can claim a trick. She takes both cards and places them together, face down, close to her. Then it is the other player's turn. The player who can claim the most tricks wins.

Variation: Show the children how to play a sorting game by themselves; as they match a picture with the corresponding letter card, they turn the trick over. Many children enjoy playing this form of "solitaire."

15. SNATCHING GAME. How to play: Use the same deck of cards as you did in the Matching Game, only this time keep the letter cards and picture cards in two separate piles. Put the letter cards face down in front of one child. Shuffle the picture cards and put them face down in front of the other player. Now both players simultaneously turn up their top cards and watch carefully for the two cards to match. The first one to see that a letter and a picture match, yells out the sound name of the letter, snatches the other player's card, and claims the trick. The player who has the most tricks wins.

Variation: The first player to slap his hand on the table to indicate that a match exists and then identify the letter by its sound claims the trick.

16. GO FISH. This game can only be played with two players.

Preparation: Use the same deck of cards as you did in the Matching Game.

How to play: Shuffle picture and letter cards. Deal five cards to each player. Place the rest of the cards, face down, in a deck before the players. (If the players are seven or older deal seven cards.)

The first player should ask the partner, "Do you have the letter *f* (for example) or a picture whose name starts with /f/?" If the second player has the requested card, she must hand it over. The first player then has a trick which he places face down in front of him. If the second player does not have the card, she says, "Go fish!" The first player then takes a card from the deck in the middle of the table. If this card matches one of the cards in his hand, he also has a trick.

The players take turns asking. The player who has the most tricks wins.

17. LETTER-TRACING GAME WITH THE STOP-AND-GO CUBE AND PICTURE CARDS. Preparation: Take a large die and cover two sides of it with red construction paper (or color them red with a magic marker). Cover the other sides with green paper (or color them green). Prepare a lined sheet as you did for previous Letter-Tracing Games, only this time prepare a second sheet for another player. Use the most recently learned letters, but not more than four in any one game.

How to play: From your collection of picture cards, pick those that start with the sounds corresponding to the letters you are going to practice. Shuffle the picture cards and place them face down in front of the players. Now one child takes a turn throwing the die. If the green side is on top, it means "go!" and she can turn up a card, say its name, and trace the corresponding letter on her sheet. Then it's the other player's turn to throw the die. If it should land with the red side on top, it means "stop!" and he loses his turn. The player who first finishes his or her sheet wins. This is a favorite of children who concentrate on playing. They don't seem to realize how often they have traced a given letter.

Almost all children commonly reverse *b* and *d, p* and *q,* and *g* and *p* since they "look alike" for a very long time. If the children have forgotten the name or shape of any of these letters, have them look it up and check it with the letter picture card. Don't ever supply the answer. If the children recheck the name with its letter picture card, they are rewarded with the confidence that they can figure out each letter's sound on their own.

In persistent cases of *b* and *d* reversal, a supplementary technique a teacher or parent can use is to draw a large, clear *b* on a sheet of paper and hang it over the child's bed for a time. The *b* has a "*belly.*"

Children can draw or paste on construction paper pictures of objects whose names start with /b/. In a different room, say the kitchen, hang a piece of paper with the letter *d,* but alter its configuration as shown below, so that it is not solid. It is now completely different from the *b* and also serves to remind children of its letter picture, the duck.

Experience has taught me that many children take a disproportionately long time to learn the first four to six letters. As they get the hang of it, they learn each successive letter faster.

After the first ten letters have been mastered in the first readiness book, you may wish to use the second readiness book, *More Sounds and Letters,*[1] in which the children will learn all the lower case letters and the digraphs *ch, th,* and *sh.* In the digraphs the sound heard at the beginning of each word is recorded by two letters which, when put together, form a new sound. At the end of this book, the capital

[1]See Appendix for publisher.

letters are introduced, since we use capital letters at the beginning of sentences and proper names.

Opportunity for freehand writing is offered here on almost every page. However, adults can write in the letters faintly for those children who need to trace them.

Parents and teachers can use the games described in this chapter as a supplement to the workbook or by themselves. Each game is used as easily with capital letters as it had been with lower case letters.

In teaching capital letters, introduce four capital letters at a time, using the sequence of letters outlined at the end of this chapter. Print each letter on one half of a 3″ × 5″ index card. Place these letters under the corresponding picture cards. Then play the letter-tracing games.

SUGGESTIONS FOR CHILDREN WITH DIFFICULTIES

Many children have difficulties in developing a proper sense of direction. Therefore, they have a tendency to form letters by starting at the bottom instead of at the top, and by going from right to left. For children who have such difficulties, try the following games.

❏ Using Raised Letters[2]

Suppose a child has trouble forming *f* correctly. Have the child trace the raised letter *f* several times. Be sure she starts at the top and goes to the bottom. Then she must go from left to right when tracing the line across the letter. Place the raised *f* in front of the child and say, "If I say a word that starts with /f/, you may trace the raised letter. If I say a word that does not start with /f/, you may not move your hand."

❏ Making a Sound Book with Larger Letters

For children with special learning difficulties, large size letters have proven helpful. Use the same size letters that you used in the letter picture cards, that is, 1¼″, 1¾″, and 2″, respectively.

[2]Raised letters may be purchased from Touch Teaching Aids—Lower Case Letters, Childcraft Education Corporation, 20 Kilmer Road, Edison NJ 08818, or lowercase plastic letters with magnets (#5073) may be purchased from Educators Publishing Service, Inc., 75 Moulton Street, Cambridge MA 02238.

As described before, help children make a sound book by drawing two lines 1¼″ apart on a blank page. Write the letter the children are practicing faintly in pencil. Emphasize the starting line with a heavy magic marker (see figure 9.3).

Let children trace each *m* with their fingers. Make sure that they start at the top and go across from left to right.

❑ Variations of Letter-tracing Game with Larger Letters

Put another sheet of two lines of *m*s in front of each child. Say, "If I say a word that starts with /m/, you may trace one *m*. If I say any other word, you may not move your pencil." If the children make a mistake, they must stop and tell you a word that starts with /m/. The first player who traces all the *m*s wins.

For another variation, use the stop-and-go cube or a color wheel to give each child a turn tracing letters.

Children who experience real difficulty in developing eye-hand coordination and a sense of direction enjoy these two variations of the Letter-Tracing Game so much that they never complain about the tracing activity even though the task is extremely difficult for them.

❑ Using Letter Pictures as Aids in All Games

Some of my pupils feel so unsure about their ability to discriminate between two letters that they need the security of constantly being able to check the letter picture cards. I place the letter pictures of the letters children are unsure about behind them so that at any time they can turn around and check the sound of a particular letter. If

Figure 9.3 Trace the letters. (This is the beginning of the child's sound book.)

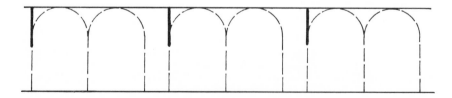

Figure 9.4 The lowercase letters, indicating the sequential movement of pencil strokes

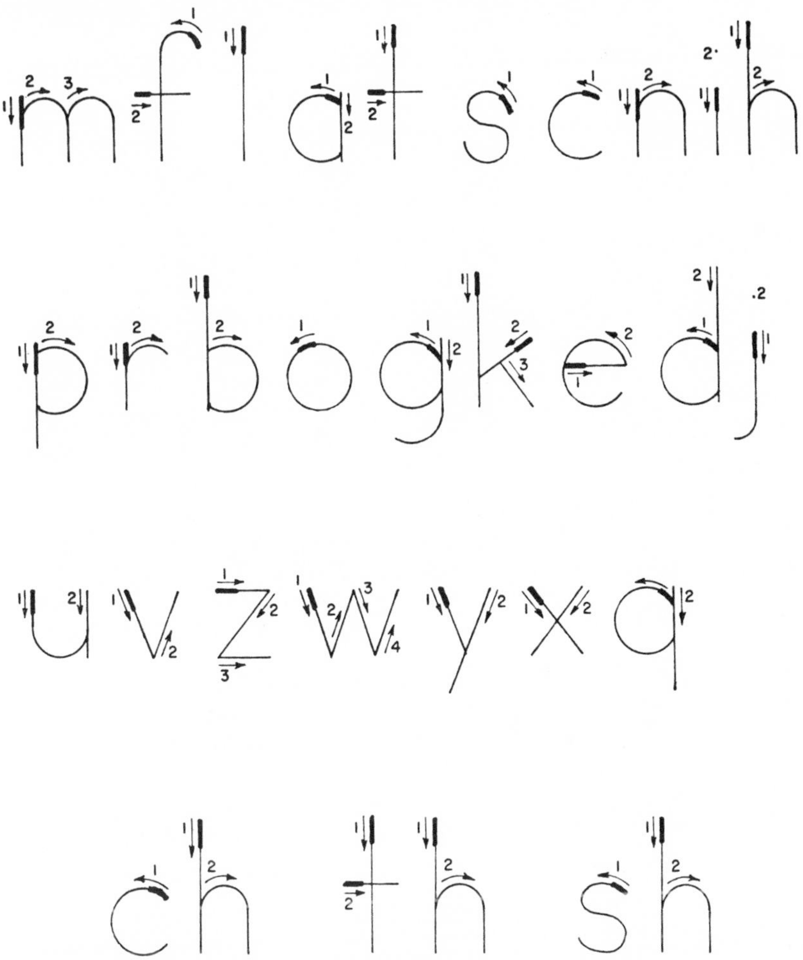

you have wall space, I suggest you tape the letter picture of the letter the children have just learned on the wall.

❑ Helping Children Write Their Names

Some children continue to write their names backward. Don't correct them by telling them they are wrong. Unobtrusively dot the name on a piece of paper and mark clearly with a red crayon where the name starts. If you let this error slip by, it will be harder to correct it later on. As a tracing game, have them go over it the correct way.

Figure 9.5 The capital letters, indicating the sequential movement of
pencil strokes

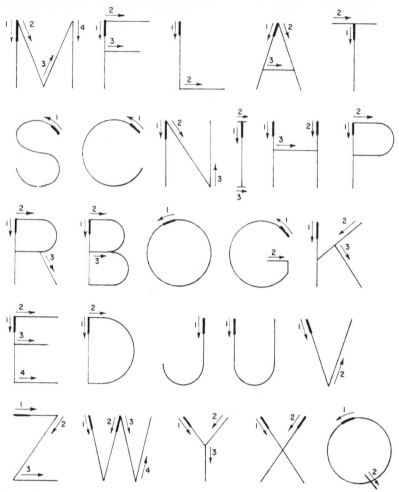

❏ When Not to Increase Play Time

Neither teachers nor parents should increase the play time they
spend with children just because the children have difficulties learning a letter. Teachers and parents must be patient. Any concern or
pressure defeats the real goal of helping children gain a feeling of
competence in an area of difficulty.

There is time. Once children have mastered two letters, they
have learned far more than just two letters. They have understood
two facts: first, letters record sounds; and second, letters face a definite direction and have to be formed in a specific way. Their under-

standing that letters record sounds is the important result of your teaching, not the number of letters they know. This insight is crucial for their success in learning to read.

❏ Stop if These Suggestions Do Not Work

Parents should stop playing these games with their children if they find themselves saying "That is wrong" or if the children balk at playing even the simplest games outlined above. They should not continue, but they also should not give up. At this point, they should probably have the child's learning difficulties evaluated as I suggested in chapter 5.

SEQUENCE OF LETTERS AND SUGGESTED PICTURES FOR EACH LETTER

/m/	magnet, mirror, marble, milk bottle, mop, mailbox, monkey, mouse, mitten, magazine, matches, mask
/f/	feather, fork, football, fan, fish, fishing rod, finger
/l/	lemon, lion, lamb, ladder, lipstick, loaf, lid, letter, lime, leaf, lollipop, lamp, leopard, lettuce
/ă/	ax, anchor, ant, apple, ambulance, astronaut
/t/	telephone, towel, toothbrush, tie, tent, tomato, turtle, teapot, top, tiger, toothpaste, table, turkey
/s/	sandwich, saw, sailboat, soap, salt, seal, sock
initial /k/ spelled c	cup, cap, candle, curtain, carrot, cake, camel, cat, cane, can, cape, cookie, candy, corn, comb
/n/	nest, net, needle, napkin, nut, nail, nurse, numerals, newspaper, necktie, note, nickel
/ĭ/	igloo, inch, Indian, ink, insect

/h/	hat, hose, hammer, hen, hanger, heart, house, horse, horn, handbag, helicopter, hand, hoe
/p/	paper, perfume, pizza, penny, pin, pail, peacock, pie, puppet, pipe, pelican, paintbrush
/r/	raccoon, raisin, ribbon, radio, rope, rake, radish, robot, rocket, rose, rooster, ring
/b/	beads, bicycle, box, belt, bat, boot, ball, bell, balloon, book, buckle, bee, bib, basket, bowl
/ŏ/	olive, ostrich, otter, ox, orchid, octopus, orange
/g/	gum, garage, golf club, guitar, goose, gift
initial /k/ spelled *k*	kangaroo, key, kerchief, king, kite, kettle, kitten
/ĕ/	egg, elephant, elf, envelope, Eskimo
/d/	doctor, dish, daisy, duck, doughnut, dime, domino
/j/	jacket, jump rope, jacks, jam, jar
/ŭ/	umpire, umbrella, Uncle Sam
/v/	vinegar, vase, violin, violet, vest, valentine
/z/	zebra, zoo, zinnia, zero, zipper
/w/	wagon, wigwam, windmill, watermelon, wallet, wishbone, web, witch
/y/	yo-yo, yak, yarn, yardstick, yolk
/q/	quail, quilt, queen, question mark, quarter (coin), quotes
/ch/	chick, chocolate, chimney, church, cherries, chipmunk, chain, cheese, checkers
/th/	thistle, thermometer, thimble, thorn
/sh/	sheep, shovel, ship, shoe, shell, shirt

10
Reading, Writing, and Spelling: One Learning Process

The step from mere sound-letter matching to reading presents a new phase in the reading process—one that needs guidance. Many children who try putting letters together on their own may attempt reading by sounding out words letter by letter: /m/ /ă/ /n/. Although they can put sounds together, they do not really understand the meaning of the word.

One of the signs that children are ready to go on to reading is that they begin to sound out words whenever they can. Another is that they begin writing words by putting letters together.

In the beginning, introduce children only to the reading vocabulary specified in this chapter. Don't teach them to read from books that contain words spelled irregularly no matter how easy and attractive they look to you. Presenting children with words like *say, far, ball, away,* and *said,* in each of which the letter *a* has a different sound, makes it extremely difficult for them to figure out on their own a new word containing the letter *a*. Stick with regularly spelled words like *cap, hat, pan,* or *bag,* in which *a* has the same sound each time. Once children have decoded a few of these words, they will discover that they can read words with a similar structure on their own. Children themselves are quick to realize their newly won decoding power, as the following comments show:

Robin (5:4) read by transfer a new word: "/Ră/ /n/? Ran! Oh, he *ran* away. I never did that before. I read it! I read it!"

Bruce (5:9) had just read five short-*a* words on his own. He was breathless with excitement. "This is a lot better than reading fake words like I do at home." Questioned as to what he meant by fake words, Bruce explained that his mother would show him words in the book she was reading aloud to him and he would "read" the words back to her.

From the beginning, reading, writing, and spelling must be taught together as integral parts of *one* learning process. As soon as children have read the word *man,* they should write it by recording the sounds they hear. In fact, writing words naturally reinforces reading. It makes sense to children that they learn to spell as the natural counterpart to reading. Furthermore, they want to put into writing what they want to say, and they are keenly aware that spelling, like reading, means figuring out.

> When Lisa (6:3) had to record the word *nap,* she turned to me and said, "I always think before I write," and then proceeded to say the word *nap* to herself, recording each letter as she heard it.
>
> A few months later, Lisa wrote *tug* on her own. She looked at the word she had written and burst out, "I know how to spell! I know how to spell!" She wrote five words on her own in her workbook, commenting, "It was magic. I wrote all the words, and I didn't have any words to look at."

Children can learn to read, write, and spell words simultaneously *only* if linguistically regular words such as *cat, hit, dog, tub,* and *jet* are used for beginning instruction. Children must first be helped to understand the structure of each group of words governed by a specific vowel and then led to read these words fluently.

Children can learn to write and spell words as easily as they say them *only* if they have neither been taught the alphabet names of the letters nor been exposed to oral spelling bees. All spelling must consist of writing down the dictated words.

There are enough linguistically regular words in the English language to give children a firm foundation for both reading these words and also spelling them. To teach children irregular words such as *come* and *where* is analogous to teaching a foreign language by introducing all the exceptions along with the rule. Obviously, such a practice would interfere with the learning of the rule. Similarly, in learning to read, write, and spell in English, children should at first learn only the general rule governing the structure of related words.

In the Structural Reading Program, the structure of the short-*a* words is taught first. Pictures are used to represent specific spoken words. Children say the name of the picture out loud, *man,* then decode the printed word underneath. Since they have just heard themselves say "man," they read *ma* as a unit, then only have to add the ending, *n.* Immediately, after children have read the word *ma - n* in two parts, they must read it again, this time fluently, putting the word /man/ into the context of the spoken language. They are asked to tell what the word means. They might say, "He is a daddy." Or

"He is not a mommy." Decoding through this one-step blending process leads to comprehension and fluency much faster than blending the three discrete letters, *m-a-n.*[1]

In the Structural Reading workbooks as well as in the games in the beginning decoding phase, words are printed with a noticeable gap between the main parts and endings of words. This gap facilitates decoding; it is far easier than reading whole words all at once.

In the Structural Reading Program, color is used to accentuate the structure of each word: vowels are printed in red and consonants in blue. Printing the vowels in red highlights the difference among words such as *pan, pin,* and *pen.* The terms *vowel* and *consonant* are not used in the beginning, but the decoding is greatly facilitated by having the vowels stand out.

Reading approaches such as the phonic and sight approaches teach word families to explain the structure of words and to speed up children's reading. They are asked to look at the *an* in *man* and then to substitute *f* for *m* to be able to read the word *fan.* This dangerous procedure requires children to focus on the *ends* of words and then to go back to the beginning. I have found that this teaches reversals.

In contrast, rhyming is pedagogically sound, for it requires children to pay attention to the structure of whole, related words.

It is true that the vocabulary consisting of short-*a* words appears rather limited, if not dull. It would be impossible to write an interesting story, for instance, with only short-*a* words. However, in the following scenario, I will demonstrate that this first impression may be deceiving.

The first grade at the Eighteenth Avenue School in Newark, New Jersey, had finished pages two and three of *Children Discover Reading,* Book B of the Structural Reading Program, when in walked twenty-nine graduate students and their professor to observe how a linguistic reading program works. The inexperienced teacher took one look at their skeptical faces and handed the class over to me.

I took the top group first, announcing that we were not going to use the workbooks today. Loud voices were heard with objections such as, "But we like our books." Unwavering, I wrote the five words of page four (Book B) on the board. Protests were heard again: "We haven't had those words. Mrs. T. didn't teach us those." Quietly, I replied, "Try to sound out each word." Every child not only sounded

---

[1]It was Catherine Stern's (my mother's) idea to put its picture above each printed word, thus helping the children read the main part—*ma,* for instance—as a unit. This procedure avoids the difficult two-step blending process *man* that caused the downfall of all phonics approaches.

out the words but was able to put each into a sensible sentence. I then erased the words and dictated them to the group. Not a single mistake appeared on their papers! The children were jubilant. "We wrote each word without your help! We did it without the workbook!"

The professor asked me to take the second and third groups consecutively. Much slower and far less fluent than the first group, every child in those groups also sounded out the words, put each into sentences, then wrote the words dictated to them. "That's really something," one of the children commented.

During the discussion period, various graduate students discussed what they had learned. One commented, "The vocabulary *hat, cap, bag, nap,* and *pad* is meager and looks dull, but what is so exciting is the fact that the children could read and write new words like *gas* and *map* on their own." Another graduate student remarked, "For the first time, I saw that what mattered is not the *content,* but the learning *process.* These children could apply what they had understood to brand new words . . . and they were so excited about it!"

The difference between content and process is crucial to understanding the different approaches to the teaching of reading. If children really *understand* the structure of words, then they can *apply* this understanding to the reading, writing, and spelling of new words.

Since that memorable experience I have taught my own graduate students to always examine the learning process and not to be carried away with the content. In reading, for instance, they should not be waylaid by the colorful signs and charts decorating a first-grade classroom. Children may simply have memorized what they say. Only if children are able to use their understanding in the learning process can they transfer this knowledge to new tasks.

The following episode illustrates the important consequences of transfer. The principal of the Eighteenth Avenue School in Newark asked me to be the reading consultant for the first grade on the lowest exponent. I agreed on one condition: I also wanted to be the consultant of the brightest class.

He answered predictably, "Why? The bright kids always learn with *any* method."

To which I responded, "But *how* they learn to read will make a difference in their attitude not only toward reading, but toward themselves. They'll see themselves as more intelligent."

Mr. N. gave in, but I think only because he needed my help for the slowest class.

The bright class proceeded on wings! The amount of transfer and consequent pride was unbelievable. In the middle of the second readiness book, some of the children "invented" writing, putting individual letters together and making words. All of these words were triumphantly recorded on the chalkboard. We had to rush the class through this second readiness book, so we could start on the first decoding book. We wanted them to learn reading and writing together as one learning process.

In the middle of the second decoding book, the children discovered the structure of words ending in a final, silent *e*. At that moment, the children took off doing nine or ten pages on their own each day. Mr. N. was speechless when he came to observe. Not only did the children read pages to him, in an unrehearsed performance, but they were bursting with excitement over their reading power.

Many of the preschool students in my private practice had such poor visual discrimination that they could learn to read only through tracing and later writing. I have included a word-tracing game for each lesson with preschoolers. Not only do word-tracing games help develop the children's writing skills, but they also develop fluency in reading words. In such games, children must scan the page to find the word asked for. This practice in scanning helped every preschooler to fluency in reading.

Teaching preschoolers spelling, however, is one of the real joys in this approach. Since they have never been exposed to a spelling bee, they can spell new words by transfer before they are taught these words in the workbook. Given an opportunity for transfer, these preschoolers would comment again and again, "Don't tell me how to spell the word. I can figure it out all by myself."

If reading and spelling is taught through insight into the structure of words, children not only demonstrate an amazing ability to read and write *new* words, but they also have a much better chance to *remember* than children taught by rote. Since the children did not learn by memorizing the "looks" of words, they can reconstruct words, in case they have forgotten them.

I was sent to P.S. 175 by the superintendent of that district. He assigned me as consultant to the slowest first grade. The principal always greeted me in the hall, but did not once set foot in "my" class. It was obvious that the entire school, headed by Mr. L., was convinced of the value of the sight method. Even when the superintendent came and expressed his delight with the children's progress, Mr. L. did not show up.

You can imagine my astonishment when, the following October, Mr. L. phoned me and requested four workshops for his kindergarten and first grade teachers.

"How come?" I managed.

"Well," Mr. L. admitted. "Your first grade was the only one that remembered all the words you taught them. They scored higher than the top group."

Some children with exceptionally good visual discrimination and memory have poor eye-hand coordination when they are four or five. These children often pick up reading almost effortlessly, but they have great difficulty in holding a pencil correctly, and thus they shy away from writing tasks. Often teachers and parents do not encourage them to write words, believing that "they'll catch up." Unlike walking and talking, eye-hand coordination, at least after children are four, depends largely on continued, carefully planned practice.

The following excerpt from a case study illustrates how important it is to teach reading, writing, and spelling together.

From 1975 until 1977 I was a curriculum consultant at an American Montessori School in New York City. One day, the teacher of the four-year-olds called me into her classroom to evaluate Johnny. At that time Johnny was not yet four; according to his parents and teacher he had taught himself to read. Indeed, he read excerpts from an *I Can Read* book that he had not seen before. When I asked him to trace lines for me in the first Structural Reading workbook, he refused. "I don't do that!" he stated emphatically. "I'm no good at it."

At the follow-up conference with parents, teacher, and principal, we discussed whether to leave Johnny alone until he "became ready" to write or whether to teach him now to trace and, eventually, to write. My urgent advice was not to let the discrepancy between his amazing reading skill and his inability to write grow. I recommended that Johnny start on *Children Discover Reading*, Book B of the Structural Reading Program. Even though he would already know how to read these words, he should go through the tracing and writing practice to develop proficiency in writing.

My argument was that by first grade Johnny would probably be reading books on the third grade level, but at the same time he would only be beginning to write the letters of the alphabet. Predictably, Johnny would then really go on strike. I volunteered to teach Johnny Book B in the form of games so his initial reluctance to write would diminish.

Very slowly, Johnny learned to hold a pencil correctly; gradually he learned to trace and, later, to write words. From the beginning, he enjoyed the tracing and writing games. By first grade, Johnny could write sentences and even short paragraphs as well as the rest of the top group.

If schools were to stop teaching reading by sight and spelling by memorization and instead teach reading, writing, and spelling together, each learning process would reinforce the other. As pointed out before, we adults do not try to read new words by sight, nor do we spell unfamiliar words by reciting the alphabet names of the letters. We sound out new words, in reading as well as in spelling.

My preschool pupils who were taught to read through careful decoding realized for themselves what learning to read means. At times they may impatiently guess at a word by looking at the picture, but when I quietly pointed to the word itself, they were thrilled to find out that they have the reading power to correct their errors. That this insight occurs even at this beginning stage is shown by the following excerpts of my pupils' records. I recall vividly how excited Robin, Lisa, and Bobby became when they were really reading without my help.

Robin (5:3) was working in Book B. Impatiently she looked at a picture, then guessed, "Chocolate sundae." Quietly I pointed to the printed word underneath the picture. This time Robin decoded the word, "*ja- m*, jam!" Then she commented, "I didn't read it at first. I just guessed, but I have to read. If I guess, I won't know how to read."

Lisa (6:1) was also working in Book B. At one point she took a quick guess at a picture and said, "Rug." I pointed my pencil to the printed word underneath and Lisa read, "*Ma-t, mat!*" Then she added, "Toni, the picture looks like a rug, but the word doesn't. I have to read the word."

Bobby (5:9) was working in Book B and guessed from a picture that the word said "tank." When I pointed to the word underneath the picture, he corrected himself, "*ga-s, gas!* The word says gas. Now that is reading."

Six months later Bobby turned to another page in Book B while studying on his own. As he attempted to figure out the first line, he commented, "You cannot always tell from the picture. You really can't. But you can always tell from the writing. You can figure out what it says."

I venture to guess that if proponents of the various sight method approaches were to analyze the comments of all the children quoted in this book, they might withdraw their objections to accurate decoding. According to these five-year-olds, guessing is *not* reading!

The vast majority of English words have a correspondence between the sounds of the consonants and the letters by which they are transcribed. True, the English vowels are by and large unpredictable, and these irregularities have to be learned. But these exceptions, including those of irregular consonants, are no reason for treating spelling like a series of unconnected telephone numbers.

Children themselves want to know how to spell words. Even when they are assured that the spelling does not matter when they write a story or a book report, they feel blocked if they can't spell.

Many years ago, friends asked me to test their eight-year-old son Chris because he had done so poorly in creative writing in school. When Chris came into my study, I asked him to tell me about his summer vacation. Chris gave a lively, descriptive account. I then asked him to write it down. The result was a short, rather dull résumé, incredibly different from his oral report. "You wrote that using only words you knew how to spell?" I asked him. He nodded. After a year of spelling lessons there was a notable difference in Chris's writing. Twenty-eight years later, Chris has obtained his Ph.D. in English at an Ivy League university—and his first book of poetry has just been published!

To sum up: If, from the beginning, children are taught reading, writing, and spelling together, they not only learn to read better, but they also learn to write well. In support of this view I present two stories written by second graders, both of whom were taught with the Structural Reading Program from kindergarten on.

The first one was taught at P.S. 39 in New York City (figure 10.1). It does have spelling and punctuation mistakes, yet it shows a good spelling foundation. The second story was written in an El Paso, Texas district where all the children came from Spanish-speaking homes (figure 10.2).

The self-confidence that results from knowing how to read, write, and spell words by transfer is as rewarding as the children's actual achievements in those areas.

> Felicia, a first-grader at the Eighteenth Avenue School in Newark, looked over my shoulder as I was scribbling down notes one day. "You are so unfair, Mrs. Gould," said Felicia disapprovingly. "If you'd print those words, I could read them."

Figure 10.1   Victoria's story

Victoria   Class 2-402
P. S.3aM anttan   February 2 4, 1 9 66.

When I Was Little

When I was little I had many toys.
And I played with my two sisters and my
brother. I had 2 dolls and 3 balls. My sister
was Madelyn and my other sister was
Lucy and my brother is victor. My
brother is little he is a little funny baby.
When my brother goes to sleep he snores.
He snores so much that I wake up. Now
I have a doll her name is sweet tammy.
I like a puppy for me and my sisters
and my brother. We like a puppy very much.
If I had a puppy I was very glad. When
I was little I was preety. I was fat but
now I am skinny. Whe I was little my
Mother tuck me to the park all day. I
liked to eat some apples oh they are so
good. When I was little I was young. I
liked all kind of food m they are very
good. I like my mother very much.
And I lik my Father very much too.

Figure 10.2 Elvia's story

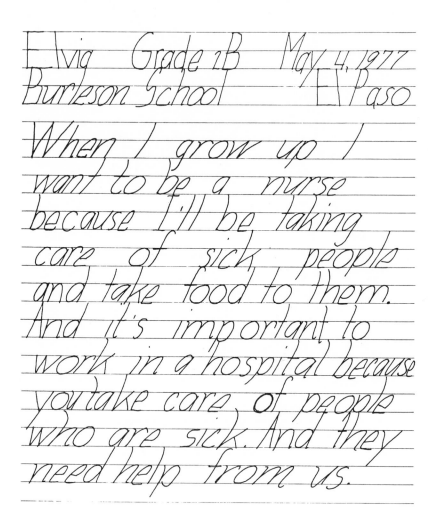

Elvia Grade 2B May 4, 1977
Burleson School   El Paso

When I grow up I
want to be a nurse
because I'll be taking
care of sick people
and take food to them.
And it's important to
work in a hospital because
you take care of people
who are sick. And they
need help from us.

11
Reading, Writing, and Spelling Games

At this point, I suggest that classroom teachers and parents may want to use *We Discover Reading,* Book B of the Structural Reading Program. A workbook that has a logically sequenced vocabulary and presents tasks to be solved will facilitate your teaching.[1] In many schools, children who have not finished a workbook by the end of the school year are allowed to take it into the next grade. This works very successfully. You can individualize your teaching by using some or all of the games described in this chapter.

For the next activities and games, collect a great many pictures from magazines, catalogs, or inexpensive picture dictionaries. The pictures should be no larger than 2½″ × 3″ (one half a 3″ × 5″ index card). Suggested pictures are:

hat	fan	pad	map	gas	rag
man	bat	pan	bag	cab	sat
cap	mat	can	jam	nap	ran
cat	rat	ham	tag	dad	van

It is advisable to have at least four or five clearly identifiable pictures for each of these words so you can make several games. You may find it simpler to draw or trace them than to cut them out. You can use the same picture five times, that is, have five identical pictures of a cat. The games that follow introduce children to their first reading of words.[2]

[1]Your children will enjoy going through *We Discover Reading,* Book B, and *We Read and Write,* Book C, of the Structural Reading Program (see Appendix). After these workbooks, the children will be able to read any book at first or even second grade level.

[2]Much of this material is covered at great length in the Teacher's Guide to *We Discover Reading,* Book B of the Structural Reading Program. See Appendix.

1. RIDDLE GAME TO INTRODUCE /Ă/ WORDS. Preparation: As always, start with spoken language. Guide the children into the next phase of learning, which is the analysis of spoken words. Instead of concentrating on initial sounds, show them how to break spoken words into main parts and endings, for instance, /mă/-/n/. Paste six pictures of objects or animals whose names contain short *a* on 3″ × 5″ blank index cards. Use pictures suggested in the list above. Stand them up before the children.

How to play: Now pronounce the name of a picture in two distinct parts (e.g., /hă/-/t/) and ask the children to indicate which one it is. If they point to the correct picture, they can take it as a trick. On another day have the children take turns asking for pictures in the same way. Continue with this game until the children are used to this new procedure.

2. WORD PICTURE CARDS. Preparation: For this game you need to make a new set of cards, with pictures that represent /ă/ words and the corresponding words underneath them. Paste one picture on a card, for example, the picture of a man, then write the word *man* underneath, leaving a gap between the main part *ma* and its ending *n*. Print the consonants in blue and the vowels in red (see figure 11.1).

How to play: Place the set of word picture cards face down in a pile. Ask one of the children in your group to pick up the first card, for example, the picture of a *cat*. Explain that in all of these reading games, in case of disagreement, they have to accept your definition of a picture since each of the pictures stands for a specific spoken word; that is, they must accept that it is the picture of a *cat*, not a *kitten*.

Have the child repeat the name of the picture on the card (cat). Now invite him to read the word underneath. He'll probably read it in two parts: /că/-/t/. Immediately afterward have him read the word again and tell you what the word means; this time he'll read the word fluently, in one piece ("Cat! It's an animal that meows. I wish we had a cat.") If the child has read the word correctly, he can keep the card as a trick. Then the next child takes a turn drawing a card.

From the very first, children put the word they have read back into spoken language, proving that they have understood its meaning. Thus, they come to realize that reading means two things: decoding a word accurately and comprehending its meaning. For the next few

Figure 11.1 Word picture cards

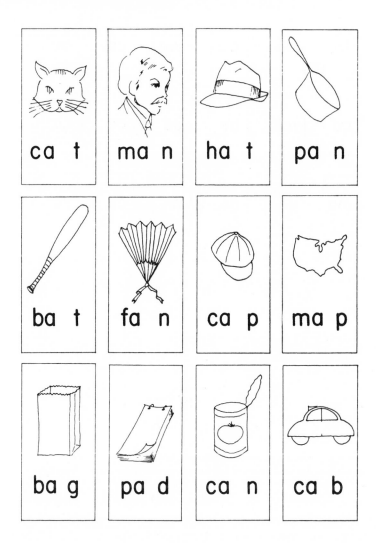

days, play only this game, adding three new word picture cards each day. Then they are ready for the next games.

3. PICTURE CARDS WITH WORD DOMINOES. Preparation: For this game use the picture cards that you made for the Riddle Game to Introduce /ă/ Words. You will also need word dominoes (see figure 11.2). You can cover standard dominoes with white labels and write a main part on one domino and the ending on the other.

Figure 11.2 Word dominoes

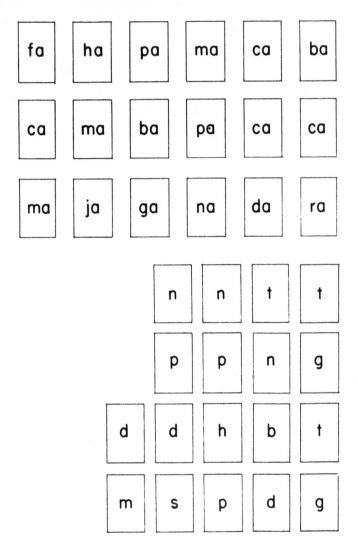

How to play: Place the main-part dominoes (such as *ca, ma, ha,* and *fa*) face down above the spread-out picture cards. Put the word dominoes bearing the word endings face up to the right side of the picture cards (See figure 11.3).

As children turn up a main-part domino, they read it in one flow; for example, they say /mă/ then find the card where it belongs, in this case, the card with a picture of a man. They place the domino *ma*

Figure 11.3 Using picture cards with word dominoes

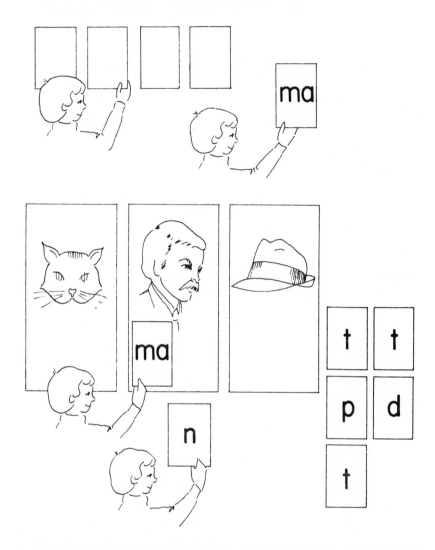

below the picture, and scanning the word-ending dominoes, pick out the appropriate ending to complete the word *man*. Have children build all of the words on the cards.

The word dominoes are an effective tool in teaching reading because they help children to read the main part of a word (e.g., *ma* or *ca*) in one piece. With this kind of practice, children learn to read words with greater comprehension and fluency. Building words with the word dominoes is also good preparation for spelling. It helps children practice the "thinking" part of spelling without the added task of writing the letters.

4. DOMINO AND FOLDER GAME. Preparation: On each inner side of a manila folder paste six pictures of /ă/ words, which you prepared at the start of this chapter. Sitting next to the children, lay the folder on the table between the children. (For optimum results, this game should be played with two children; it can also be played with four, two on each team).

The side of the folder in front of each child is her or her side to play on. Now place the main-part dominoes face down along the top of the folder. Divide the word endings between the children and place them face up on each side of the folder.

How to play: After children have identified each picture in the folder, they pick up a main-part domino, read it as a whole, then see if they have a picture it fits. For instance, they turn up *ca;* if they have the picture of a cap, they put the domino on top of the picture. They should then say /cap/ to themselves and hunt for the *p* among the endings. Very soon children can play this game without your help.

After all the words have been built (covering up the pictures), call for a domino word by a simple definition or riddle (for example, "What goes on your head?"). The children have to scan all the words they have built to find the one you asked for.

5. PICTURE LOTTO WITH WORD DOMINOES. Preparation: Use two 5″ × 8″ blank index cards as master cards. Draw six equal squares in pencil on each card. Paste one of the /ă/ pictures you prepared at the beginning of the chapter on each square (see figure 11.4). Each master card should have different pictures.

How to play: Each of the two players should have a master card in front of him or her. Put the main-part dominoes face down above the cards. Line up the endings, face up, at the sides. The child chosen to be the caller turns up a main-part domino and names it. Then comes the excitement: which of the two players can first claim it as her or his card? Whoever has claimed the main-part domino now looks for the proper ending to complete the word. The player who has first built all the words on her or his master card wins.

Figure 11.4 Master card with six picture cards

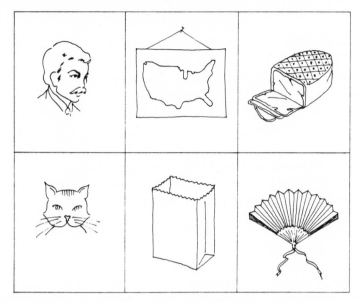

Variation: Many children enjoy playing lotto as solitaire. In this case, give one child both master cards, place the word dominoes in position, and let the child build the words for the pictures on both cards.

6. PICTURE CARDS AND WRITING WORDS. Preparation:

Make a set of ten picture cards representing /ă/ words. This time don't write complete words underneath. Instead, prepare writing lines and write only the main part of each word (see figure 11.5).

How to play: Place the picture cards face down in front of the children. As they turn up each card, they name its picture (man), read the main word part underneath (/mă/), and say the name of the picture again, this time emphasizing its ending (man). They then complete the word underneath the picture by recording the /n/ they hear. Finally, have them read the whole word back to you before they go on to the next cards.

Variation: Write *ma, ca, pa* on lined notebook paper:

ma _____
ca _____
pa _____

Figure 11.5 Picture cards with word parts

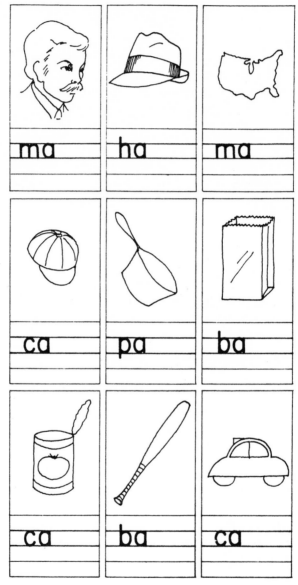

Give a riddle for the main part of a word. For instance, "This is the beginning of a word that tells you how to find your way to a new store" (map). The children must guess the word, then write its last letter.

Variation: Again write *ma, ca, pa* on lined notebook paper:

ma _____

ca _____

pa _____

This time the children have to think of a word that begins with *ma* and think up an ending to complete a real word.

These two variations have been very helpful for children who were taught to blend the first two letters rather than to read them as a unit. Furthermore, they enjoy both variations.

Children will very soon ask to write entire words on their own. At this point I would let them choose a colored folder at the stationery store. Draw sets of four lines on unlined paper (see figure 11.5) and write their names on their first Writing Book. Let them illustrate the cover if they wish. Each time they finish a writing game, let them put their papers in their folders. They can illustrate each word if they wish.

7. WRITING GAME WITH TOYS. Preparation: Prepare sheets of paper by drawing sets of four lines, leaving ample space between the sets.

Collect in a large paper bag toys or objects whose names represent /ă/ words, for example, a fan, pad, bag, hat, cap, cat, map, man, can, jam, bat, rag, and bag.

How to play: Give children the prepared sheets of paper. Have them shut their eyes and touch a toy from the bag. Let them guess what it is, then, eyes open, take the toy out and check whether they are right. Then ask them to record its name on their sheets of paper.

As a preliminary step, they can build each word with the word dominoes if they want to.

8. WRITING GAME WITH THE STOP-AND-GO CUBE. Preparation: Use the stop-and-go cube as described in chapter 9. Have the bag of toys and the word dominoes ready. Give children prepared sheets and pencils. Play this game with two to eight children.

How to play: The children take turns rolling the die. If it lands on green, they may, with closed eyes, pick out a toy from the bag and write its name on their sheet of paper. If the die lands on red, they lose their turn and another child rolls the die. The player who has written the most words wins.

As before, children may first build each word with the dominoes, then write it.

Children enjoy this game immensely and ask for it repeatedly.

9. WRITE DOWN WHAT IS MISSING. Preparation: Give each child a prepared sheet of paper with sets of four lines. Have a tray ready with toys or objects representing /ă/ words.

How to play: Put five of the objects on the tray. After a child has looked at everything on the tray, have her close her eyes. Take one object away. The child can now open her eyes, figure out what you have removed, and write down what is missing. She will read it to you so you can both check the answer.

After a while, one of the children will want to take a toy away for you and you will have to write down what is missing. Be sure to print the words clearly; do not use cursive writing. Use red for vowels and blue for consonants so each child can easily check your paper. (The children, however, are never asked to write the words in red and blue.)

10. RIDDLE GAME AND WRITING WORDS. Preparation: Rule pieces of paper as before.

How to play: Give one sheet of paper to each child. Make up a simple riddle whose answer is a short-*a* word, for example, "You need this to find your way in a strange city" (map). Have the children guess the riddle, then record the word.

If a child insists on giving you a riddle, place before the child a set of pictures representing /ă/ words and say that the riddle has to refer to one of these pictures.

11. WHAT IS MY NAME? Preparation: Play this game with two children. On blank 8½″ × 11″ paper, mark six squares in rows of two each. The children paste a picture representing an /ă/ word in each square. Draw four lines under each picture. Have the stop-and-go cube ready.

How to play: One child throws the die. If it turns up green, the child can write the name for the first picture on the page. If it turns up red, it is the other child's turn to label a picture. The player who first labels all six pictures wins.

Many children enjoy labeling the pictures on their own without playing a game. They may even ask for more pages to do.

Variation: Leave out the pictures and instead print six words very faintly under each of the blank spaces. Have the children read each word, go over it with a pencil, then draw their own picture in the blank above the word. Their drawings should be commended and not corrected.

12. WORD-TRACING GAME. If I were allowed to teach only one game, this would be my choice. Not only does it provide practice in tracing (which so many children need as reinforcement), but it also gives practice in reading fluently. Children learn to scan a list of words until they find the right one. Fortunately, this is also one of the most popular games with the children.

Preparation: Play this game with two children. Have ready a deck of picture cards representing /ă/ words. With faint pencil lines print half of these words on one piece of paper that you have lined, and print the remaining words on another piece of paper. Give each child one of the papers.

How to play: Shuffle the picture cards and place them face down in a pile between the two children. The first child picks up a card, reads the word, then scans the words on the sheet. If the word is on his sheet, he traces over it with the pencil. If it is not, he puts the picture card in a discard pile. Now it is the other child's turn. The game ends when there are no more picture cards in the original pile. The player who has written the most words wins.

Variation: This is another game that works well as solitaire. Print the words lightly on a piece of paper and give a child the corresponding picture cards. The child turns up each picture, finds the word on the paper, and traces it. The game is finished when the child has written all the words.

Variation: When children can read these words fluently and trace them with ease, you can turn this game into a spelling and writing game. Distribute lined notebook paper. Now as players turn up a picture card, they must write the corresponding word, that is, spell it.

Variation: Use this game with children who do *not* need tracing practice. As you call a word, the child has to find it quickly and cross it out. The child gets two points for every correctly crossed-out word. You get two points for every word the child misses.

If the children have misspelled a word in any of the games, don't correct them. Encourage them to read the word back to themselves. They can correct their spelling error by proofreading the word, again and again if necessary. In this way children develop independent skill and increase their confidence in their own spelling ability.

The card games in the next group are designed to help children proceed from careful decoding to fluent reading. Eventually they'll be able to glance at a word and grasp its meaning.

As a general preparation for the card games, cut 3″ × 5″ index cards in half. Paste one picture representing an /ă/ word on half of a card, for example, a picture of a bag. On the other half, print the corresponding word, in this case *bag*. At this point write the word *bag* as a whole unit without leaving a gap between the main part and the ending. Print the consonants in blue and the vowels in red, as usual.

13. MATCHING GAME. Preparation: Play this game with two children. From your collection choose fourteen picture cards that represent /ă/ words and their corresponding word cards.

How to play: Shuffle the cards and place them in a pile face down in front of the two players. One child turns up the first card, for example, the picture of a man, and leaves it face up in front of her. The other child picks up a card, for example, the word *cat*, and leaves it face up in front of him. If the first child now turns up the card with the picture of a cat, she can match the word card and take the first trick. If the child should turn up the card with the word *man*, she would match her picture card of a man and also have a trick. The children take turns until there are no more cards. The player who has the most tricks wins.

Variation: This game can also be played alone. Shuffle the cards and place them face down in front of the child. As she turns up a picture card, she puts it to the left. As she turns up a word card, she places it to the right. Whenever she sees two cards that match, she pairs them as a trick, continuing until all the cards are matched up.

14. SNATCHING GAME. Preparation: Use the previously described deck of cards that contains picture cards and matching word cards.

How to play: Play this game with two children. Place the word cards face down in front of the children. Shuffle the picture cards and also put them face down in front of the children. Now both children simultaneously turn up the top card, watching carefully to see if the two cards match. The first child to see that a word and a picture match, yells out the word, snatches the other player's card, and claims the trick. The player who has the most tricks wins.

15. WORD LOTTO. Preparation: Play this game with two children. Use eighteen 3″ × 5″ blank index cards; they will be the master cards. Draw a vertical line down the middle. On the left side of each card write an /ă/ word using red for vowels and blue for consonants. The right side stays blank. It will be covered with the corresponding picture.

Now cut nine index cards in half. On each half, paste a picture corresponding to each of the eighteen words, and on the reverse side write the word that names it.

How to play: Spread out nine master cards in front of each player. Now place the word cards face up between the two children. One child reads aloud the word, for instance, *cat*, then turns the card over to look at the picture and check that he has read the word correctly. Whoever has the master card with the word *cat* claims the picture and puts it on the blank space of that card. The first player to fill all nine master cards wins.

As the children look to see if they have the particular card needed, they have to scan all the words. This develops their ability to read the words fluently, at sight as it were.

Variation: This game can also be played alone.

16. WINNING WITH TRICKS. Preparation: Play this game with two children. Use twelve /ă/ word cards and their corresponding picture cards, which you prepared earlier.

How to play: Shuffle the word cards and put them face down in front of the children. Deal the picture cards alternately and have the children hold the cards in their hands. Now one child turns up a word card from the pile and reads it. If the child has the corresponding picture card in his hand, he puts it on the table with its word card as a trick. Now the other player picks up a word card to see if she can make a trick. The player who has discarded all of the picture cards first, and thus has the most tricks, wins the game.

Variation: This game, too, is popular as solitaire.

17. GO FISH. This game can be played best with two players. In this case, I am going to play it with two fictitious children, Robin and Jed.

Preparation: Use the same deck of cards as you used in the Snatching Game.

How to play: Shuffle the picture and word cards and deal five cards (of seven cards in the case of an older child) to each player. Place the rest of the cards face down in front of the players.

Robin now asks Jed, "Do you have the word *fan*?" If Jed has this word card, he must give it to Robin. If he doesn't, he says, "Go Fish." In the latter case, Robin takes a card from the deck. In either case, Robin must put the trick down in front of her.

Now it's Jed's turn to ask Robin for a card. If Robin does not have the desired card, she tells him to "Go Fish."

The player who has the most tricks wins. The children choose this game often as the favorite to play at the end of each lesson.

18. SLAPJACK. This is a rhyming game. Suggested rhyming sets are:

man—can	hat—cat	nap—lap	map—cap
bag—rag	ran—fan	sat—bat	pad—sad

Preparation: Cut eight 3″ × 5″ index cards in half. Write one word of a rhyming set on each half, that is, write *hat* on one half card and *cat* on the other. Continue until you have used up all right rhyming sets. Remember to write the consonants in blue and the vowels in red.

How to play: Shuffle the cards and divide them, face down, between two children. Both players turn over a card at the same time and place it next to the other player's. If the words on these cards do not rhyme, the cards become discards, and each player takes another card. If the words do rhyme, both players slap their hands on the cards. The player who slaps her hand first takes the other player's pile of discards and adds it to her own stockpile. The game ends when one player has captured all the other's cards.

As you go on with these games, some children will probably develop a favorite that they'll want to play each day. That's fine. This repertoire is simply to provide you with variety.

It is essential to stick to the short-*a* words until they are read fluently. Only if each word is read fluently can children understand *how* words in a sentence are related, and only then can they extract a meaning from the sentence as a whole.

TEACHING THE /ĭ/ WORDS

If children have enjoyed learning to read short-*a* words and urge you to teach them more, then it's time to introduce them to short-*i* words. Since the children now understand how to proceed from spoken to written short-*a* words, it will take far less time and effort for them to read short-*i* words. Such progress comes about when children are taught through understanding rather than by rote. They themselves realize how many words they can discover on their own, and a sense of achievement gives additional momentum to their eagerness in learning to read.

❑ Preparation for Word Games

Prepare new pictures for teaching the short-*i* words.
Suggested pictures are:

pin	pig	dish	pill	mix	wig
lid	ship	mill	fish	fix	dip
six	bib	hill	sit	hit	zip
kit	fin	lip	fig	dig	hip

Use the same sequence of games with the short-*i* words as you did with the short-*a* words.

Once children know the short-*a* and the short-*i* words, you can introduce them to the following new games.

19. SORTING GAME. Preparation: Play this game with two children. Take two sheets of notebook paper and draw two columns on them, each one headed by a key word, such as *man* and *bib*.

How to play: Now give a simple riddle to the children, for instance, "It is an animal that meows." The first child solves the riddle, then writes the word in the proper column. The second player then takes a turn solving the next riddle and writing it in the proper column on his paper. The child who has written the most words wins.

Variation: Choose eight of the picture cards representing /ă/ words and eight of the picture cards representing /ĭ/ words. Add four cards bearing a big red stop sign. Shuffle all the cards and place them face down in front of the players. The children take turns picking up a picture card and writing the corresponding word in its proper column. Of course, the players who draw a stop card lose their turns. The player who has written the most words wins the game.

20. THE FILING BOX. Preparation: Buy 3″ × 5″ index cards and an inexpensive filing box for each child. Each box should have two dividers with tabs on them (you can make your own by pasting gummed labels on index cards). Write *hat* on the tab of one divider and *six* on the other. Be sure the children can readily see the tabs. Choose eight picture cards representing /ă/ words and eight picture cards representing /ĭ/ words.

How to play: Shuffle the cards and place the deck face down in front of two children. One child picks up a card, says the name of the picture, then writes it on an index card lined with four lines. Encourage that child to illustrate this word simply (or to cut out a picture from a magazine or mail-order catalog and paste it above the word) and file this card behind its proper key word. The children take turns picking up cards, writing, illustrating, and filing.

Variation: When the children have filed all their cards, you can use the following variation. Ask the players to take out all of the cards. Shuffle them and place them face down in front of the players. When you say "Go!" the players must turn up one card after another as fast as they can read it, and file it behind its proper key word. Whoever has filed her or his cards first yells "Stop!" and thus wins the game. You can check how long it takes each player to file the cards. Write the time on a pad. They'll want to play the game again to improve their score. Not only do they have fun competing against themselves as well as against each other, but they also gain speed in reading these words fluently.

As each new vowel group is introduced, write its key word, for example, *log*, on the tab. Children now add the short-*o* words to their filing boxes.

Once children can read the short-*a* and short-*i* words fluently, you can introduce them to very simple sentences. Sentence reading, analogous to learning to talk in simple sentences, is a decidedly more complex process than reading single words. Children have to figure out the relationship of the words to each other in order to extract the meaning from the sentence as a whole. The first sentences children read will be very simple.

INTRODUCING SENTENCES IN SPEECH

Teach children the difference between an incomplete sentence, such as *my blue sweater*, and a complete sentence, such as *Anne has a blue sweater*. Explain that in writing we put a dot, called a period, after a complete sentence, and we start the first word of the next sentence with a capital letter. Don't dwell on this. Children do not need to remember the term *period* or even to understand the concept of a complete sentence. They will learn these in first grade. You are merely preparing them for learning this later.

To read simple sentences, children need to read the words *has* and *is*. Always introduce new words in a spoken sentence. Hence, use the words *has* and *is* in sentences, then write them, using blue for the consonants and red for the vowels. Have children read each word and use it in a sentence.

Introduce the article *a* in an oral sentence, saying, for example, "Mom has *a* pencil." Then write the article *a* down in black. Children will realize that it looks like the short vowel *a*. Explain that since the *a* sounds slightly different from the pure vowel sound heard in *man* or *can*, you print it in black. You are going to write all irregular words in black.

Follow the same procedure with the article *the*. Use *the* in a sentence, then write it in black. The children know *th* from the letter picture cards. Explain that the schwa sound heard at the end of *the* is recorded by *e*.

21. NONSENSE GAME. Preparation: You can play this game with four children. Cut 5″ × 8″ index cards into one third and two thirds each. Write one of the following subjects on each of the smaller size cards, and one of the predicates on each of the larger size cards.

Dad	has ham.	The fish	has a cap.
Sam	has a fish.	The hill	is in the pan.
Ann	has a pad.	The pig	has a bib.
The cat	has a bat.	Jill	is in the can.

Shuffle the subjects and place them face down in one pile. Do the same for the predicates.

How to play: The first child picks up a subject, then a predicate, reads the sentence, and decides if the sentence makes sense or if it is nonsense. If it is nonsense, the child can keep the cards as a trick. Then it is the next child's turn. Again, only if the sentence makes no sense can the child keep the two cards, subject and predicate, as a trick. The player who has the most tricks wins.

22. MAKING A NONSENSE BOOK. Preparation: Put several blank sheets of paper in a folder for each child. Let the children decorate the covers. Write on each folder the title *My Nonsense Book*.

How to play: Let the children trace the title and add their names. Now write one simple nonsense sentence at the bottom of each page. Let each child illustrate it. Figure 11.6 shows a sample page from Mia's (6:6) nonsense book.

TEACHING OTHER SHORT-VOWEL WORDS

If the children want to go on, teach them short-*o*, then short-*u* and finally short-*e* words. The vocabulary for each new group is listed below.

Short-*o* words:

mop	top	dog	ox	rock	hop
pot	cot	log	doll	dot	lock
fox	box	rod	fog	dock	sock

Short-*u* words:

mud	run	tub	tug	sun	bud
nut	hut	cup	bus	bug	bun
rug	gum	jug	cut	pup	cub

Short-*e* words:

bed	wet	well	men	net	leg
ten	pen	set	pet	bell	egg
hen	red	get	jet	den	peg

Figure 11.6   Page from Mia's nonsense book

For each new group, prepare a set of pictures before you start teaching. Use the same sequence of games as you did with the short-*a* words.

As children's reading vocabularies expand, the Sorting Game, Filing Box, Nonsense Game, and Nonsense Book will, of course, become more interesting.

At this point children can read, write, and spell about ninety words, and they can read simple sentences that contain linguistically regular words. This is a solid foundation on which children's future reading skills will develop. More important than the number of words is the children's awareness that real reading means accurate decoding *and* the comprehension of a particular word. Thus, they have begun to understand the learning-to-read process. This is far more important than the number of words or the content of what they can read.

This is a good point at which to stop, especially if children are going to first grade. You have started the children on learning to read through understanding the structure of each word. Their confidence that they can read words on their own is as important a stepping stone to reading as the decoding skill.

SUGGESTIONS FOR CHILDREN WITH DIFFICULTIES

Sentence reading requires fluent reading of the words that make up a sentence. Therefore, when I observe children who do not read words fluently, usually the first group of short-*a* words, I do not let them go ahead in their workbooks. Instead, I use tracing and writing games exclusively until they have achieved fluency in reading single words.

The most important tools for helping children read fluently are the tracing and writing games (for example, game 12, Word-Tracing Game). The repeated scanning required in the games has helped my most disabled students attain fluency in reading a given group of words.

A SIMPLIFIED VERSION OF GAME 12, WORD-TRACING GAME. Preparation: Prepare a sheet of paper for each player. In faint lines, write words from two or three vowel groups, for example, *hat, kit,* and *lot*. Distribute the papers among the players.

How to play: The first player throws the stop-and-go cube. If it is green, the neighbor has to dictate a word from his paper to the player who threw the cube. The player then scans his paper and traces the corresponding word. The player who has written the most words wins.

This game helps children discriminate between similar words (for instance, *hat, hit,* or *hot*) besides aiding fluent reading and aligning words.

Variation: Pick out all the picture and word cards from the groups learned so far, for example, /ă/, /ĭ/, and /ŏ/ words. Use sheets of paper as described above. If a child picks up a word, perhaps *pad*, a second time, she scans the words and then says, "I can't use *pad*. I already traced it." This child then gets another turn.

This version is extremely popular with children and thus should be used frequently to help them learn how to read new words fluently.

COLUMN GAME WITH THE STOP-AND-GO CUBE. Preparation: Two to eight children can play. Give each player a sheet of paper with five columns, each headed by a word representing the groups learned so far, for instance, *cat, pin, mop, mud,* and *pen*.

How to play: Combine the picture cards from all the vocabulary groups into a deck, and place it and the stop-and-go cube in front of the children. One player turns up a card, says the name of the picture, finds the column where the word belongs, and writes it in its proper column. Each word counts one point; the player with the most points wins the game.

This game is helpful in spelling as well as in reading. Let one child dictate and the other children write the words. The child who dictates must scan the words on each child's sheets so no word is used twice.

RHYMING GAME. This is a simpler version of the Slapjack Game described earlier.

Preparation: Use the same deck of cards you prepared for Slapjack.

How to play: As players turn up a card, they must write a rhyming word on their paper. Each word counts as one point. The player who has the most points wins. This game helps children read and write words.

REUSING A PAGE. All of the children I have helped in the classroom or privately have benefited from the simple technique of *reusing* a page. For instance, after they have read the words on a page, I ask, "Quickly, can you find the word *man*? . . . the word *map*?" and so on.

Questions can also be asked about a paragraph or a story the children read. Scanning a page for a definite word or idea helps their fluency grow immensely.

12
Advantages of Early Intervention

The educational authorities of our times are divided, by and large, into two major camps. On one side exists the opinion, voiced in the educational section of the *New York Times* 13 April 1986, that early learning and schooling are extremely important. On the other side, parents are cautioned to wait until their children get ready for learning to read; in other words, until they are mature enough to be able to understand the learning process. Above all else, teachers and parents are told not to push children.

In teaching four- and five-year-olds to read, I have found that children with learning disabiities need an earlier start than so-called average children in preparing them for learning to read. At the pre-school level they have the interest and, not insignificantly, the free time for it.

It would be ideal if pre-kindergarten and kindergarten teachers combined forces to develop a systematic, structured readiness program. As I said before, it does not matter *how many* letters children learn, as long as they learn to understand how sounds are recorded by symbols, and that symbols, unlike pictures and objects, are often differentiated by their direction (see page 43).

In the case of severely learning disabled children, it would be economical, both in time and money, to have reading specialists on the staff of our elementary schools solely for diagnosing and reme-diating four- and five-year-olds. One-to-one tutoring is an effective way of helping children learn to read and write. Specialists know how to adapt learning tasks to challenge children without frustrating them. Such early intervention would decrease illiteracy enormously.

Many teachers and parents will, at this point, raise the question "Why *tutor* four-year-olds? Wait! They have plenty of time to learn." The answer is that a number of these children could learn to read by the middle or even the end of first grade if they were tutored intensively then. However, such a postponement is risky. Since maturation in itself does not cure the disabilities, uncorrected problems are compounded at the *beginning* of first grade. In a classroom where children are not divided into groups, children who make reversals (such as writing a letter backwards), who start mirror writing, or who read words backwards are not easily noticed by the classroom teacher. Thus, they frequently make errors and reinforce tendencies that become ever more difficult to break.

Even with a warm, sympathetic, and accepting teacher, a nonthreatening classroom, and a totally relaxed and noncompetitive atmosphere emanating from both teacher and parents, the children themselves are the first to see that other children catch on more quickly and progress to reading books while they are still struggling with the first letters. Feelings of inadequacy and failure damage their self-image and harm their natural motivation to learn. Too often the learning pattern set in first grade continues for the rest of their school lives. At this point, every parental suggestion is interpreted as meaning "Mom and Dad have to help me so much because I'm no good." The resulting feelings of anger and inadequacy interfere with *all* learning.

It has been devastating to me to observe that even very bright children who did not learn to read in first grade considered themselves failures by the end of the first grade. In all my notes the following sentence reoccurs, "I am stupid. I did not learn to read. The others did."

Not only is failure damaging to the children's self-esteem, but it significantly decreases their motivation to learn. I am convinced that early success experiences in learning to read would prevent tens of thousands of high school students from dropping out of school.[1]

Working with preschool children who have not yet developed deep-seated negative feelings about their abilities is always easier. Hence my urgent plea for early intervention!

It is essential to remember that I am advocating learning through playing rather than through applying pressure. I am suggesting twenty-five to thirty minutes a day for readiness activities which leaves the rest of the day for creative activities.

As proof, I could present over two hundred excerpts of case stud-

---

[1] In March 1991, Representative Thomas Foley, Speaker of the House, in a speech on TV, expressed his concern that half of all seventeen-year-olds can't read the newspaper and, subsequently, can't perform the jobs they should be able to. Early intervention would certainly be *one* way of turning seventeen-year-olds around!

ies. The majority of these are older remedial students. (I define *remedial student* as any child from first grade on who has experienced difficulties in school.) A minority of my students have been preschool and kindergarten children who were diagnosed, either by an outside expert or by myself, as having learning disabilities. Without exception, the latter group never experienced failure in reading, writing, or spelling.

These preschoolers were taught exclusively by a sensible approach that allowed them to understand the structure of linguistically regular words. I deliberately gave them tasks that permitted them to read and write words by transfer. These opportunities for transfer generated the excitement of discovery and invariably increased their intrinsic motivation. Not one of these children ever felt pushed, as I could prove by numerous transcripts.

Knowing how to read in first grade has given these children a head start over many of their contemporaries. Children themselves know the value of this skill early on: "I can read, so I am smart." Since they have felt successful in as crucial an area as reading, they are more willing to try learning math, for instance, where they will probably also need more time and effort than most of their classmates.

In contrast, my remedial students experienced frustration and failure in their classrooms and thus developed an intensely negative self-image. Their motivation decreased. School became a place where "no matter how hard I try, I am not as good as the others." Such hurts heal gradually and only after students have caught up with the achievement of their peers.

A reading specialist, stepping in *after* children have experienced failure, is faced with the double job of remedying the lack of reading and writing skills and also helping children overcome their feelings of discouragement. I am convinced that all of my remedial students were as eager to learn and as confident of making progress as the preschoolers who had the fortune to receive early help. What irony! We shield children from pressure at the age of four or five only to allow them to fail, by the thousands, at the start of first grade.

The following excerpts from my records provide strong evidence of the success of early intervention. The first five children had serious learning disabilities but were tutored at the age of four or five and therefore never experienced failure. In contrast, the excerpts of the last four children show that, sometimes as early as kindergarten and first grade, children may develop deep-seated feelings of inadequacy that interfere with the ability to learn.

My preschoolers were able to learn to read through independent discovery and thus developed confidence in their ability to learn and think. The children's comments will give you an understanding of how successful such children can feel.

❏ Arlene

Arlene came to me the summer before she entered public school kindergarten; she was not quite five. She was referred to me by a psychiatrist who was concerned that she had a very poor self-image and an extremely low tolerance for frustration. In addition, she had been diagnosed as having a serious perceptual problem. Because of these and other difficulties Arlene had had the unique misfortune of being "flunked out" of nursery school.

Arlene could not have been taught by her parents for many reasons. She had three older brothers and a younger one so close to her age that the rivalry between them was intense. No amount of parental attention seemed to have helped her feelings of jealousy and insecurity. In addition to the family structure, she was not an easy child to teach. At four and a half she had developed such negative feelings about herself that she had a very low tolerance for frustration. At the beginning of our sessions, she greeted every task with, "That's too hard. I can't do that." It took a lot of patience to teach Arlene, for I had to judge each time whether a task or a game was really too hard and should be simplified, or whether with quiet but firm support Arlene could handle it. Not only did Arlene learn to read before entering first grade, but when she realized that she could read new words on her own, she burst out, "Oh, I'm so clever!"

❏ Bobby

You will remember Bobby from chapter 3 as a child with tremendous learning problems. His parents, in particular, had noticed his poor motor coordination: he had difficulty catching a ball as well as holding a pencil. His mother realized early that she could not help her own child get ready for reading. "I wasn't able to teach him to hold a pencil. . . . I had to back out. He was so resistant. . . . He just won't listen to directions. He wears me down."

The father expressed his concern that Bobby would not try anything unless he could do it well.

Bobby and I started working together when he was four years and seven months. For two years we met once a week for an hour. Bobby's visual discrimination was slow in developing, slower than that of any other children whose records I use in this book. In the course of eight months Bobby really *knew* only eight letters, but he never felt discouraged about his learning. Because he was allowed to check each letter with its letter picture card rather than having to ask me for its name, he felt a sense of growing accomplishment, which gave rise to a spurt in learning. He mastered the remaining sixteen letters in six months.

It has been my experience that this happens frequently with children with learning disabilities. It takes them a very long time to develop the visual discrimination necessary to identify the first letters. Once they have developed the skill and have understood the learning process, they learn the remaining letters far more quickly.

Bobby, like most children with poor visual discrimination, felt most successful in writing. Because of all the tracing practice, he developed a kinesthetic feeling for the letters: his muscle sense seemed to direct his hand in forming the letter, almost like learning Braille. Bobby's eagerness to practice writing and spelling helped him to finally master all the letters.

When Bobby began to read words, his poor visual discrimination again slowed up his initial progress. It took him three months to master (that is, to read fluently) the short-*a* words and two months to master the short-*i* words. No school could have afforded Bobby this much time to practice. Yet here, too, with concentrated practice, he learned to read these words fluently. Moreover, as he realized he was reading words without my help, he became increasingly confident. A year and a half after we started work, every one of his comments showed his feelings of competence. (His age in parentheses before each comment shows the intervals at which his learning occurred.)

(6:0)

When Bobby completed a difficult page, he looked absolutely radiant. "I can say the words now. Boy, am I smart." (He explained that he meant, "Now I can read them in the same fast way as I am talking.")

Bobby refused help with a new word. "I want to be on my own. I don't like people helping me."

(6:2)

"These words are easy. You know, reading is so easy."

(6:3)

When he pressured me to start a new page, he said, "Let's go. You know I'm good at it. Here we go."

He worked steadily, again noting, "I figured it out all by myself." Our final session ended with the following dialogue:

Bobby: "What do they do in first grade on the first day? Teach you how to read?"

Mrs. G.: "I don't think so."

Bobby: "It won't be hard for *me* when they do."

☐ Lisa

Lisa was brought to me at the age of four years and eleven months. Her parents reported that her early development had been slow. Lisa had been tested by a psychologist, and the IQ score on the performance test was markedly lower than the one obtained on the verbal test. Her combined score, from both verbal and motor tests, was average. I asked to see Lisa for two evaluating sessions.

I found that Lisa listened well; she was able to follow directions, and she obviously enjoyed the individual attention, encouragement, and praise. Her attention and concentration span were excellent; she was not ready to go home after the full hour of either visit. She moved quickly from not seeming able to hear initial sounds of words in the first session to being able to identify them in the second. But Lisa showed extremely poor eye-hand coordination, and her sense of direction was weak; she traced every circle in the wrong direction, although I first demonstrated with my pencil which way to go. Her visual perception and memory were poor.

It seemed to me that, like Bobby, Lisa could overcome a great many of her learning difficulties if someone worked carefully with her and allowed her to proceed at her own pace. In such a way she would not experience failure.

Not long after we had begun working together, Lisa was tested in school and found to have a perceptual impairment. She was slated for a special ed. first grade composed of children with learning disabilities.

During her kindergarten year Lisa was given special help from an adjunct teacher twice a week in addition to working with me twice a week. Lisa was five years and two months old when we began. She appeared eager to work in the Readiness Book, which she remembered from our preliminary sessions. When Lisa spontaneously asked for a "new letter," I introduced the letter picture card for /f/; remembering the learning process perfectly, she said the word *fan* slowly to herself, then added, "So the letter says /f/."

For a long time Lisa had difficulty tracing *m* in the correct direction. I gave her additional practice. She followed my finger tracing *m*; then she traced it on her own with her finger several times; only then did she trace the dotted *m* with a crayon. Interestingly enough, she was about to start tracing the second *m* starting at the bottom and to the right when I stopped her and pointed with my finger to the beginning. For the next two months my finger would show Lisa where to start and unobtrusively prevent her from going in the wrong direction.

(5:5)

Lisa can identify ten letters and she is exuberant about her success. When I introduce the harder version of the Mail Carrier Game to her, using plain letters instead of their letter picture cards, Lisa comments, "It's harder this way, but I can do anything I want to do."

Yet at this same time her tracing was still poor. She enjoyed the Letter-Tracing Game because it was a game in which she could beat me. When I hesitate where to write my letter, Lisa teases, "I was faster. I'm pretty smart . . . smarter than you."

(5:6)

Lisa wants to try to write straight letters freehand, without my dotting them for her first. "I can do it all by myself," she insisted. From this time on her motivation to learn increased by leaps and bounds.

(5:9)

Her motor coordination seems to have improved. Her lines are straighter, and therefore I was able to show her how the letters are aligned with the lines and spaces on the paper. Perceiving and accomplishing this is incredibly difficult for children like Lisa. She cannot remember which letter starts at the top, which occupies the middle, and which reaches to the bottom line. It is clear she will need many months to learn to align the letters properly. However, since there was no way for her to compare her performance with that of other children, she never felt defeated but was free to evaluate herself solely in relation to her own progress.

(5:10)

Lisa can read her first words without my help. During this memorable session Lisa would look at me from time to time with wonder and happiness: "I can read, Toni. I really can. Did you hear me?"

Her first writing of whole words shows that she had no difficulty in spelling them (see figure 12.1). Obviously, her only difficulty was in aligning the words properly in space. In fact, I dictated words she had not yet been taught: *sat, fat, ran, mad*. By repeating the words to herself and slowly listening to each sound, she was able to write them by transfer because she had thoroughly understood the encoding process. Lisa is very pleased at being able to write these words. "I can think it out," she comments.

(5:11)

There is a trend, from lesson to lesson, toward fuller and more significant definitions. Whereas in the beginning Lisa did not use full sentences, she now does. At one point when we played the Word Writing Game, Lisa asked me, "Should I write a capital or a real one?" The implication that capitals are not real letters struck me as a delightful indication of her originality.

Her increased verbal facility was noticed at home. Her mother said, "Lisa talks about everything at home. She asks about everything. She just seems more intelligent."

(6:1)

Lisa's mother stopped in to report that Lisa is now trying to read everything in sight. Overnight she has begun asking her parents to

Figure 12.1. Lisa's writing progress

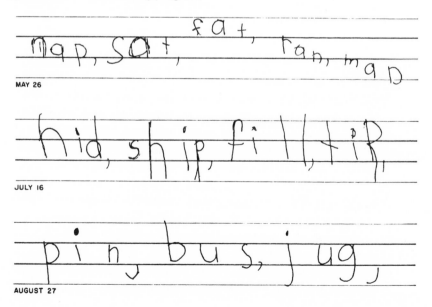

tell her words that she cannot figure out by herself. A few days later Lisa spotted the date on my notes. "I can read it. It says August."

(6:2)

Lisa can write words without one spelling mistake and she can align the letters properly. Eleven months of constant writing practice was bearing fruit. Lisa's coordination had becme stabilized, and her ability to align letters properly had become very much more reliable (see figure 12.1 for her progress).

Lisa's improvement showed up in school, where a psychologist tested her again at the end of kindergarten. He no longer found a perceptual impairment and withdrew his original recommendation that Lisa be placed in a special first-grade class for children with learning disabilities. Instead he recommended that Lisa be placed in a regular first grade.

What is as rewarding as Lisa's catching up and developing strength in her areas of weakness is her motivation to read. But because children like Lisa have lived with real success, they read constantly, as confirmed by the parents. The following dialogue proves this point:

Mrs. G.: "What do you like best in school?"
Lisa: "My teacher."
Mrs. G.: "And next best?"
Lisa: "The children."
Mrs. G.: "And next best?"
Lisa: "*Books.*"

☐ Felicia

Felicia is the middle child in a family of three children. Her siblings are outgoing and, without fail, outshine Felicia, who seldom volunteers an answer or a smile. I saw Felicia for the first time at the end of her nursery school year. In evaluating Felicia I found that she was intelligent. Her eye-hand coordination and sequencing skills were excellent.

When Felicia first entered my study, she did not look at me. She barely spoke above a whisper, the phrases she did speak were syntactically faulty, and she pronounced many words incorrectly. Felicia countered any question I asked with "What?"

In summary, I realized that Felicia's deficits were her inadequate language skills, her poor auditory and visual discrimination, and a rather meager fund of information for her age. But she had the motivation to learn. Her parting question was, "When do I come back?"

For weeks, Felicia struggled to learn the difference between the letters *m* and *f*. Because neither Felicia nor I had any time pressure, she had all the time she needed to overlearn. Actually, Felicia learned all of the letters through tracing and writing them in games, which she enjoyed. Just looking at the letters did not enable her to remember which was which.

By the end of her kindergarten year at an excellent private school, Felicia knew most of her letters (differentiating between *m* and *n*, *b* and *d*, and *g* and *p* were still difficult for her, but this is the case for many children), and she was able to start on her first decoding book. She was thrilled. At a time when she couldn't recall her grandmother's first name or the place of the class trip they had gone to that morning, and when she still had difficulties following directions, she was able to decode a great many short-*a* words. "All of the words have /ă/ in them," she remarked. "That's so easy!"

Every step in the learning-to-read process was slow for Felicia and required overlearning. But because Felicia had started at four, there was no rush. By the end of first grade, Felicia had developed excellent handwriting skills via all the tracing games. She had progressed in developing oral language skills, but she still needed a lot of help in this area. One of the tasks Felicia found most difficult, for instance, was to incorporate two written words into a spoken sentence.

Right now Felicia is in the middle of her second decoding book. Thus, she is almost on target for second grade, which she'll enter in the fall. To sum up Felicia's progress: "I have nothing to worry about," said Felicia. "I can read."

☐ Jed

Jed was referred to me by his best friend in kindergarten, who kept advising him, "You have to go to Toni so you can learn how to read." His mother, tired of her son's entreaties and also apprehensive about Jed's lack of progress in all language skills, brought him to me.

I saw Jed twice for an informal evaluation. A handsome, outgoing boy, Jed answered every question or direction with "What did you say?" Jed did not answer in full sentences; furthermore, his pronunciation of many words was incorrect. Jed demonstrated on a variety of tasks that he had poor auditory and visual discrimination skills and that his memory in those areas was worse. Jed consistently drew lines from right to left. Yet his reasoning ability was excellent, definitely in the superior range.

Like Robin, Lisa, and Felicia, Jed struggled to learn to discriminate between *m* and *f* but mastered them by the end of four weeks. Since he invariably won (by design), Jed never tired of the tracing and writing games. Just like Felicia, Jed learned the sound-letter correspondence of all the letters, first through tracing, then through writing.

Jed enjoyed progressing to his first decoding book. Obviously, this is a thrilling experience for children who are not yet in first grade. Although Jed's memory for spoken words was still extremely poor, he could decode a great many words and give their meaning. Owing to Jed's tracing practice, his freehand writing of words became amazingly good and gained him a lot of praise from his teacher.

Because Jed's auditory discrimination was also poor, we often played the Sorting Game, mentioned in chapter 9. I used two columns but handed him a deck of cards containing words with all the short vowels. Jed had to read each card and decide which word would have to be discarded and which would fit in a certain column. "That is fun!" he commented. Figure 12.2 is an example of Jed's writing and spelling.

Jed particularly enjoyed decoding and writing words by transfer. His auditory discrimination had improved so much that he now could hear the sounds in regular words and, therefore, he could record the sounds by their corresponding letters. Recently, I dictated to him words such as *camp* and *brag* that have final and initial consonant blends before he learned these words in the second decoding book. "Give me more words, harder words," Jed demanded.

When Jed came to the page introducing words in which the final, silent *e* makes the preceding *e* long, Jed pleaded with me, "Don't teach me that page. Let me try." Effortlessly, Jed read the new words *Eve* and *Steve* on his own. "See, I can read it myself," he beamed triumphantly.

Yet in this same lesson Jed wrote a reversed *J* although his name starts with that letter. He had difficulty reading *the*, which he had seen many times before, and he had difficulty learning to read the phrase, "No, no!" probably because the exclamation mark looked to him like the letter *I*. It took two additional lessons for Jed to be able to distinguish between the exclamation mark and the *I*. In a reading workbook, Jed reversed *3*, *6*, and *9* and wrote *8* incorrectly as two

Figure 12.2 Jed's writing (Sorting Game)

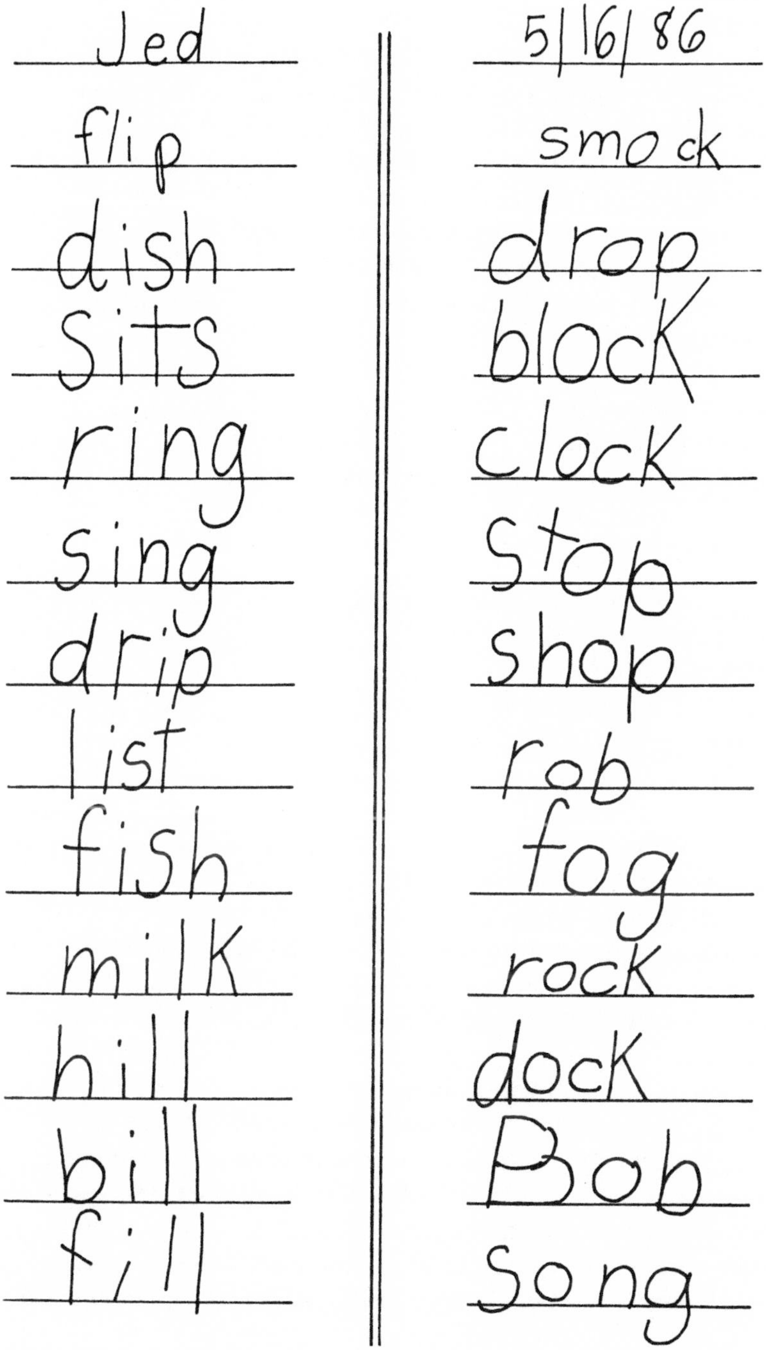

Jed

flip

dish

sits

ring

sing

drip

list

fish

milk

hill

bill

fill

5/16/86

smock

drop

block

clock

stop

shop

rob

fog

rock

dock

Bob

song

separate balls. When I asked Jed to identify the symbols, he replied, "Sometimes I am not sure." Here, too, he will need a longer time to learn the symbols than most of his classmates; he will need a great deal of overlearning.

None of these problems with direction and discrimination have prevented Jed from learning to read and spell. By the end of summer, Jed will have finished his second decoding book and thus be up to the grade two level. At this point Jed is confident that he will learn to read as well as his sister does in fifth grade—in his eyes, the pinnacle of achievement! Jed is proof that learning disabled children can learn to read, write, and spell words by transfer because they understand the structure of words at a time when their visual discrimination and memory are still poor.

I shall conclude my plea for early intervention with excerpts from four remedial pupils' records. These students were referred to me *after* they experienced failure in school.

❏ Ray

Ray was in fourth grade when I first met him. The Child Study Team at his public school had tested Ray and diagnosed severe learning disabilities, including a mild speech defect. The team recommended that Ray be placed in a special education class. Ray's parents, after observing this class, refused to accept the team's recommendation on the grounds that all the children in this class were hyperactive whereas Ray was a quiet, shy youngster. The Child Study Team acquiesced. Ray was put into a normal classroom, and the parents brought him to me for tutoring.

My own test results showed that Ray had no solid foundation for decoding, nor could he spell. Initially, he was unhappy to start his lessons with such a simple book as Book B. "That way I'll never catch up," he commented. It took months of encouragement and, more important, his realization that he was learning to read and spell before he looked and felt confident.

By the middle of sixth grade, Ray read almost at grade level, but he still read more slowly than most of his classmates. About that time, Ray asked me for help in his spelling homework. He was to study words containing a long-*e* sound, such as *meet* and *meat*. I separated the words containing *ee* from the rest of the words and used this vocabulary in card games described in chapter 11. In the next lesson,

Ray practiced only the words containing *ea.* Two weeks later, Ray bounced into my study shouting, "Mrs. Gould, Mrs. Gould, I was the only one today who got an A in the spelling test!"

❑ Tracy

Tracy's mother called me with the urgent request that I tutor her daughter. When I asked for reasons, she replied, "Tracy comes home every day from school crying, 'I am so stupid.' " Further questioning revealed that Tracy was attending the kindergarten at a public school for gifted children only. Tracy had an IQ of 155 but had not been able to learn to read as most of the other children had. I accepted her over the phone!

Tracy greeted me with the sentence, "Everyone in my class can read but I can't." I showed Tracy some sight words such as *when* and *who*, but at the end of the lesson she couldn't remember how to read these words. Then I opened up the first decoding book; I promised that she would learn to read with this book. Tracy looked dubious. It wasn't until a year and a half later that she exclaimed, "I can read now. I can read well."

In this case the prevention should have started when Tracy was four so she could have overlearned in the areas of her weakness: visual discrimination and directional skills. Tracy is a striking example—one of thousands, I am convinced—that bright children do *not* learn well with just any method. Tracy and her parents could easily have been spared a great deal of frustration and pain with early intervention.

❑ Susan

Susan has just been referred to me by an outside speech therapist; she is in the middle of first grade. On my first evaluating session, I found that Susan could not identify a single lowercase letter with certainty. She could read one word correctly: *cat.* It became clear immediately that Susan had a severe visual perceptual handicap.

I found out that Susan had been taught both lowercase and capital letters simultaneously. Susan's inventory memory had rebelled and she had retained neither letter form.

Susan has a very poor sense of direction: she reversed letters as well as words. For all these reasons, she had been kept back in kindergarten, a fact that did not do much for her self-confidence.

From the beginning, I realized that Susan's verbal intelligence is above average, since she is able to hold a clear and concise conversation with me. However, Susan did not think so. Her ever recurring remark was, "I am really stupid."

In our first lesson, I showed Susan the letter pictures; she lit up. "I can look up each letter by myself." In six lessons, she has learned to read all the short-*i* words. She has started to decode the short-*o* words.

Susan will learn to read, within a couple of years, and hopefully regain her self-confidence.

☐ Neil

Neil's parents had heard of me through friends of theirs who were child therapists; the parents brought Neil to me for an evaluation when he was finishing first grade. The results of tests administered to Neil at school showed that he had done very well on a prescreening test prior to first grade, and scored very high on the *Wechsler Intelligence Scale for Children* (WISC). Other tests had diagnosed neurological difficulties: Neil had a sequencing problem, could not connect his visual with his auditory memory, and had grapho-motor difficulties.

From my own evaluation, I concluded that Neil's assets were his high intelligence and his verbal skills. His speaking vocabulary and sentence structure were roughly three years ahead of his chronological age.

As usual, I gave Neil relatively easy reading selections to read aloud from and kept a record of his errors. I show only the very beginning of his record below.

Reads	Should Read
is	live
at	in
find	live
this	the
think	thick

From this small sample of errors, it was apparent that Neil had no foundation for decoding. Neil needed my assistance to read the irregular word *who*. After coming across this word six times on the same page and asking for assistance, Neil asked me the seventh time, "What does this word say?" It was obvious that he would have continued to have problems learning to read by the sight method.

From the beginning, at least once during every lesson, Neil made comments such as "Everyone has learned to read but me. . . . My hand didn't do what my head wanted it to do" (this comment was in reference to a misspelled word). . . . "Do you think I'll ever learn? . . . Will I be able to read hard books some day?"

If Neil could have been tutored when he was four years old, he would never have had to go through the painful experience of failure. What makes this story so heartbreaking is that Neil has a marvelous, secure relationship with his parents, who have always given him a great deal of encouragement and support. If ever a child was destined to have self-confidence and self-esteem, Neil was. And he had it until he entered first grade. This competent, verbal, and bright child must have felt as if a series of thunderbolts were striking him out of nowhere when, for the first time in his life, he met with failure in first grade.

Neil is attending one of the best private schools in New York City. Who should have advised the parents to seek professional help? The kindergarten teacher in that school? Or the first-grade teacher in that same school? We can't put blame on anyone, for the teachers meant well. Hundreds of thousands of educators would agree with them: don't pressure young children either at school or at home to learn in an area they are performing poorly in.

As a matter of fact, Neil's parents remember that as late as the end of first grade, when Neil was one of the few pupils who had failed to learn to read, the teacher recommended that the parents find a psychiatrist. "Neil expects too much of himself," said the teacher. That Neil hadn't learned to read was not considered sufficient cause for emotional problems!

What a tragedy! Spare children from being "pushed" but allow them the suffering of failing. A bright child like Neil notices accurately how quickly most of his classmates can read a new word whereas he can't read it after the eleventh time. Neil would also always need *more* time to overlearn than most of his classmates.

Sadly, the parents, too, have been hurt by Neil's failure. They, like most parents, have become apprehensive and communicate this uneasiness to Neil, not necessarily through words.

Since Neil was so unhappy with his lack of achievement in *reading* in first grade, I decided (for the first time in my tutoring experience) to concentrate mostly on teaching him reading and not writing or spelling. By the end of second grade, Neil had caught up in his reading; he could read anything on the second or third grade level.

Neil's eyes sparkled when he told me that he and his mother were taking turns reading aloud *Charlotte's Web*.

As of the spring of third grade, Neil had difficulty in writing a short story or a book report even though he knew I didn't care how many spelling errors he made, for we would correct them afterwards. Figure 12.3 presents one of Neil's writing efforts, to illustrate the gigantic task that then lay ahead of him in learning how to spell. By the way, Neil was never taught to spell phonetically, either in class or by me. His phonetic spelling approach was his own device to try to remember how these words are spelled.

At the end of third grade, Neil scored only on the 15th percentile in spelling but on the 99th percentile in reading!

From the beginning, the discrepancy between Neil's verbal skills and his writing ability has been striking. Neil has the imagination and the reasoning power of a writer, but he is unable to translate his imagination and thoughts onto paper. He was not taught early in first grade to record a sentence as naturally as he pronounced it.

Neil has higher and more creative intelligence than any of the preschool pupils I have ever taught. But Neil was not given an early start.

As this book goes to press, Neil, now in seventh grade, has received all As in his first term and has just been accepted at New York City's famed Bronx High School of Science.

Figure 12.3   Neil's spelling

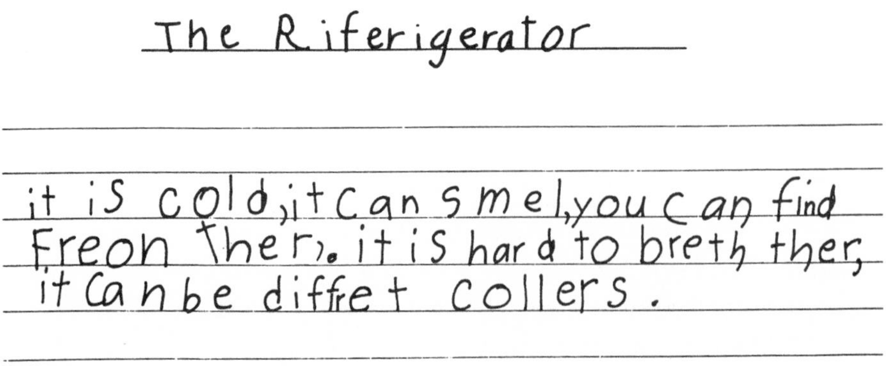

The Riferigerator

it is cold, it can smel, you can find Freon ther. it is hard to breth ther. it can be diffet collers.

Afterword: A Few Thoughts for Parents and Teachers

To a healthy young child, learning—including learning to read—is fun. Teaching children to read so that they understand the learning process kindles their natural interest in reading. They enjoy learning because their minds are working and because they are active, not passive, in the learning process.

My decision about how to teach children to read came from my examination of learning in general. Children learn most productively and economically when they have insight into the structure of learning: insight allows for transfer, for the excitement of being able to apply their learning to new tasks. Such learning is a challenge to the mind, not a burden to the memory.

In contrast, rote learning of any subject that has a structure is unproductive. Memorization gives no opportunity for transfer; it simply means learning *more* facts in order to cover the material rather than having a tool that helps in discovering new, related facts independently.

It is advisable that beginning readers learn through understanding structure. If the initial reading vocabulary is organized so that all the words are linguistically regular, children can learn to decode. In the method outlined in this book, the initial instruction follows a highly structured sequence: from careful decoding, to fluent reading of single, linguistically regular words, to reading sentences. But the structured sequence allows for each child's active discovery and individual rate of learning.

The principles of Structural Reading can be adapted to suit the special needs of individual children. Those with poor auditory discrimination can have more time, more practice, and more enrichment activities in their area of weakness. Likewise, children with poor visual discrimination are given the time, practice, and special activities they need in the initial phase of learning sound-letter correspondence to master the letters, specifically, practicing how to trace and write letters, then words.

All children, bright as well as slow, advantaged as well as disadvantaged, learning abled as well as disabled, do better when learning is intellectually logical. The brighter the students, the more able they are to generalize and to transfer their reading skill to reading words they have not been taught before, and the faster they will be able to read material of all kinds. Significantly, less intelligent pupils also do better with an approach that requires thinking rather than rote learning. Their ability to reconstruct words they may have forgotten gives them a feeling of confidence and security.

Bright children in our educational system are often neglected on the premise that "bright children will learn no matter what." True. Such children will probably learn to read. But *how* they learn at the very beginning of formal learning will have as pronounced an effect on their subsequent intellectual development as it does on the slower child. If they learn to read by using their intellectual powers in the learning process itself, then they develop increasing confidence that they are able thinkers, that they can apply their thinking to new tasks, independent of an adult.

The word *method* has fallen into disrepute among many educators who point out that other factors in teaching take priority over the specific method used. This argument is, of course, valid. A teacher's personal qualities and intuitive handling of each child are far more important to the child's ultimate learning than any particular method. Similarly, the parent's attitude, the relationship with the child, is a significant underlying factor in the child's ability to learn. It takes warm, sensitive teachers and parents to challenge children without pressuring them, to give them approval and support without criticism. Intellectually, young children must never be allowed to feel that they don't quite measure up to teachers' or parents' expectations.

Given these priorities, method assumes tremendous importance. A self-teaching approach to reading allows children to venture forth on their own while the teacher or parent serves as a helping observer. If children are taught with a method that lays visible the structure of the subject, they can learn through insight and thus develop in the learning process itself a steadily increasing confidence in their own ability to think.

It is tragic that in an attempt to shield preschool children from learning to read, many childhood experts prevent children from feeling successful in an intellectual area. For many reasons we have downplayed these opportunities in favor of success in the creative areas. Yet both are important.

As controversial as what method to use in teaching reading is the question *when* to start. Youngsters benefit most from learning at that critical time when they are at a peak of readiness. Natural readers indicate in their curiosity about printed language that they are ready to learn much sooner than most of our schools are prepared to teach them. They should not be kept waiting with the promise that they will learn to read in first grade. If the critical period is missed, children may lose some of their incentive to close the gap between their interest in the contents of books and their ability to read them by themselves. The bright youngster, at five, is simply interested in learning to read; at six, this child wants to read about rockets, the moon, or dinosaurs.

It is not advisable to let natural readers teach themselves to read; on their own they may teach themselves imperfect reading skills. Children are impatient by nature; it is quicker to guess at a word than to figure it out. Helping children discover reading prevents the habit of guessing from developing. Giving children the tools to unlock the meaning of a word lets them experience an excitement that far surpasses a haphazard stabbing at words.

An early start in reading readiness is advisable for *all* children— not to satisfy a parent's ambitions, but to gain time for children to acquire the necessary readiness skills, including some sound-letter knowledge.

Children who show less interest in reading than the natural reader should also have an early start, because they will require *more* preparation. By starting early you can take advantage of their pleasure in games and their need to have time spent with them.

Many years as a reading consultant in schools, as well as in private practice, have convinced me that a child's chronological age, after the age of four, has nothing to do with alleviating minor or major learning disabilities. *Six-year-olds take just as long to learn to identify letters as four-year-olds.*

I am not suggesting putting four-year-olds behind desks, to equip them with pencils and notebooks, and to have them write letters. I am proposing ten to twenty-five minutes be set aside as playtime for readiness activities. Learning should proceed at a leisurely pace adapted to the individual child's needs. If a child needs six weeks to learn a single letter, that is acceptable. There is time to learn at four or five!

Not only are children spared the ordeal of failing, but their parents are spared the anguish of watching their children suffer when they are not able to learn in first grade. Moreover, first grade teachers are most appreciative when children come to school knowing how to read.

It can't be emphasized enough how much early success in learning to read helps to develop children's intrinsic motivation to learn. Today's drop-out rate in high school is, in my experience at least, partially related to the lack of success in the early grades, such as kindergarten and grade one.[1]

There are, at the other end of the continuum from the natural reader, children with such pronounced learning disabilities that only a professional can help them. Early intervention is very successful with such children. Given the extra time and practice they need to learn to read, these children experience success rather than failure. Furthermore, the children's difficulties are corrected before they escalate in school.

I am not saying, of course, that all reading problems would disappear if all children were taught early. Some children have such serious neurological or psychological impairments that they may not be able to learn to read.

Nor does my plea for an early start stem from a concern that four- and five-year-olds do not accomplish enough. We can see from their comments how even children with learning problems, if started early enough, develop an increasing confidence both in their reading skill and thinking ability. They are aware that their intelligence is an important factor in learning to read.

Children should learn through thinking as early as possible, for it is the thinking and not the amount learned that will contribute to their intellectual growth. We should evaluate their knowledge by how well they can apply it to new situations or tasks. Only in this way do we allow for creativity in the intellectual areas as we do naturally in the arts.

Children who are helped to figure out words and sentences on their own will practice thinking and get better and better at it. And,

[1]In March 1991, Secretary of Education, Lamar Alexander, proposed that, by the year 2000, 90 percent of high school students should graduate . . . I suggest that one step toward reaching this goal would be to establish pre-kindergartens all over the country which, while developing emotional and social maturity, would teach readiness skills including sound-letter knowledge.

in this process of learning to use their minds and discovering that they can depend on their ability to think, they will develop an ever increasing motivation for learning more.

When five-year-old Lisa insisted that she no longer needed a certain teaching aid, she put it very succinctly, "I want the hard way. I like the thinking way. . . . That's the way to learn."

APPENDIX

Learning Materials for Reading Readiness and Reading

The Structural Reading Program
by Catherine Stern, Toni S. Gould, and Margaret B. Stern. The following components of this program can be ordered separately from American School Publishers, P.O. Box 4520, Chicago, IL 60680.

We Discover Sounds and Letters (Book A-1)
Pupil's and teacher's editions

More Sounds and Letters (Book A-2)
Pupil's and teacher's editions

Key Picture Cards
One set per classroom or family is sufficient.

We Discover Reading (Book B)
Pupil's and teacher's editions

We Read and Write (Book C)
Pupil's and teacher's editions

Learn to Read Books
by Toni S. Gould and Marie Warnke
Available from Walker and Company, 720 Fifth Avenue, New York, NY 10019. Six sets, each containing six story books for grades one to three. These books use exactly the same reading vocabulary as the Structural Reading Program. The vocabulary is specified in each book.

Learning Materials for Number Readiness

The Structural Arithmetic Program
by Catherine Stern, Margaret B. Stern, and Toni S. Gould
The following components of this program can be ordered from Educators Publishing Service, Inc., 75 Moulton Street, Cambridge, MA 02238.

The materials come in two sets:
Set A for kindergarten and grade one
Set B for grades two and three

Experimenting with Numbers (teacher's guide) for kindergarten

Structural Arithmetic—Workbook 1 (with teacher's guide) for grade one. [In press. Contact publisher for date of publication.]

Structural Arithmetic—Workbook 2 (with teacher's guide) for grade two. [Contact publisher for date of publication.]

Structural Arithmetic—Workbook 3 (with teacher's guide) for grade three. [Contact publisher for date of publication.]

Guide to Children's Books

Since any book lists become obsolete quickly, I suggest that you use the following reference books to decide which books you may want to buy or take out of the library.

Child Study Children's Book Committee at Bank Street College, 1985. *Books to Read Aloud with Children through Age 8.* Bank Street College, 610 West 112th Street, New York, NY 10025.

Child Study Children's Book Committee at Bank Street College. *1986 Edition: Children's Books of the Year.* Bank Street College, 610 West 112th Street, New York, NY 10025.

Fader, Daniel. *The New Hooked on Books.* New York: Berkley Publishing Group, 1981.

Larrick, Nancy. *A Parent's Guide to Children's Reading.* New York: Bantam Books, 1982.

In general, I highly recommend children's books that have won the Caldecott or Newberry Awards.

Books for Beginning Readers

In general, I recommend the HarperCollins *I Can Read Books,* the Random House *Beginner Books®,* the Thomas Y. Crowell *Let's-Read-and-Find-Out Science Books,* the Lippincott *Super Books,* and the Western Publishing Company *Easy Easy Reader* Golden Books.

For easy-to-read, high quality paperbacks, I recommend you get catalogs from the following publishers:

Starline Books
Scholastic Book Services
Englewood Cliffs, NJ 07632

Reader's Digest Service
Education Service
Pleasantville, NY 10570

Dell Publishing Co.
1 Dag Hammarskjold Plaza
245 East 47th Street
New York, NY 10017

Viking Paperbound Books
625 Madison Avenue
New York, NY 10022

Children's Magazines

Child Life (ages seven to nine)
P.O. Box 567
1110 Waterway Boulevard
Indianapolis, IN 46206

Cricket
Open Court Publishing Company
1058 Eighth Street
La Salle, IL 61301

Ebony, Jr.
1320 South Michigan Avenue
Chicago, IL 60616

Electric Company Magazine
Children's Television Workshop, Inc.
Department S.O. 9
North Road
Poughkeepsie, NY 12601

Highlights for Children (ages two to twelve)
2300 West Fifth Avenue
Columbus, OH 43216

Humpty Dumpty's Magazine (ages four to six; excellent for beginning readers)
P.O. Box 567
1110 Waterway Boulevard
Indianapolis, IN 46206

Jack and Jill (ages six to eight)
P.O. Box 567
1110 Waterway Boulevard
Indianapolis, IN 46206

Kids by Kids for Kids (ages five to fifteen; written by children)
Kids' Publishers Inc.
777 Third Avenue
New York, NY 10017

Sesame Street Magazine (for pre-school children)
Children's Television Workshop, Inc.
North Road
Poughkeepsie, NY 12601

Sprint (fifth and sixth grade remedial students)
Scholastic, Inc.
730 Broadway
New York, NY 10003

SUGGESTED READINGS

Adams, Marilyn Jager. *Beginning to Read: Thinking and Learning about Print* (Cambridge, MA: MIT Press, 1990). *This book is an absolute* must *for teachers; it will become the classic in this field. Those parents who need reassurance that they are doing the right thing in starting their children off early should at least read pertinent portions. I recommend obtaining the* Summary, *which contains the most important information:* Summary of Beginning to Read: Thinking and Learning about Print. University of Illinois, P.O. Box 2276, Station A, Champaign, IL 61825-2276

Bruner, Jerome S. *Toward A Theory of Instruction* (Cambridge, MA: The Belknap Press of Harvard University, 1966).

Durkin, Dolores. *Children Who Read Early—Two Longitudinal Studies* (New York: Teachers College Press, 1966).

Durkin, Dolores. *Teaching Young Children to Read,* 2nd ed. (Boston: Allyn and Bacon, 1976).

Simpson, Eileen. *Reversals. A Personal Account of Victory over Dyslexia* (New York: Pocket Books, 1979).

For Parents

Baker, Carolyn D. and Freebody, P. *Children's First School Books: Introduction to the Culture of Literacy.* (Cambridge, MA: Basil Blackwell, 1989).

Butler, D. *Reading Begins at Home.* (Portsmouth, NH: Heineman, 1987).

Farnham-Diggory, Sylvia. *Schooling.* The Developing Child Series. Bruner, Jerome S., Cole, Michael, Lloys, Barbara (series eds.) (Cambridge, MA: Harvard University Press, 1990).

Garber, S. W., Garber, M. D., Spitzman, R. F. *If Your Child is Hyperactive, Inattentive, Impulsive, Distractible.* (New York: Villard Books, 1990).

Heath, S. R. *Ways with Words.* (Cambridge, MA: Cambridge University Press, 1983).

Schaeffer, Charles E. and DiGeronimo, Therese Foy. *Help Your Child Get the Most out of School* (New York: New American Library, 1990).

Weinbaum, E. and Friedman, K. *Stop Struggling with Your Child* (New York: Harper Perennial, 1991).

Wiener, H. S. *Any Child Can Read Better* (New York: Bantam Books, 1990).

For Teachers

The first two titles are, in my opinion, a must:

Lieberman, I. Y. and Lieberman, A. M. "Whole Language vs. Code Emphasis: Underlying Assumptions and Their Implications for Reading Instruction." *Annals of Dyslexia,* vol. 40, 1990 (Orton Dyslexia Society, 80 Fifth Avenue, New York)

Robinson, H. M. "Visual and Auditory Modalities Related to Methods for Beginning Reading," *Reading Research Quarterly 8,* 1972, pp. 7–39.

Chall, Jeanne S. *Learning to Read: The Great Debate* (New York: McGraw-Hill Book Co., 1967).

Chall, Jeanne S. "A Decade of Research on Reading and Learning Disabilities." Samuels, S. J., ed., *What Research Has to Say About Reading Instruction* (Newark, DE: International Reading Instruction, 1978), pp. 31–42.

Downing, J. *Reading and Reasoning* (New York: Springer-Verlag, 1979).

Flood, J. and Lapp, D. *Language/Reading Instruction for the Young Child.* (New York: Macmillan, 1980).

Hall, N. *The Emergence of Literacy* (Portsmouth, NH: Heineman, 1987).

Just, M. A. and Carpenter, P. A. *The Psychology of Reading and Language Comprehension* (Boston: Allyn and Bacon, 1987).

Montessori, M. *The Secret of Childhood.* (New York: Ballantine Books, rev. 1966).

Orton, S. T. *Reading, Writing and Speech Problems in Children* (New York: W. W. Norton, 1937).

Wallach, Michael A. and Wallach, L. *Teaching All Children to Read* (Chicago: University of Chicago Press, 1976).

Wells, G. "Preschool Literacy-related Activities and Success in School," D. Olson, N. Torrance and A. Hilyard, eds., *Literacy and Learning: The Nature and Consequences of Reading and Writing* (New York: Cambridge University Press, 1985).

INDEX